Sept 2nd When we commit to something is it for life, when Jesus commits to something it is for life, and life ever after. Divorce exist because love is lost, Jesus will never divorce you, but you can divorce Him, you can return to easy you, easy you has no commitment in his heart, easy you was never truly commited to anything, accept Jesus Christ as your Lord and Savior and He will show you what commitment looks like, and as you understand more and more about Him you will become more like Him, He does not take away your freedoms, He inhances them, He doesn't take away anything from you, He gives you a heart that reflects His own, that heart is Love

Sept 1st You don't have to go far to see what the world has to offer just turn on the tv and watch the news, people cry for things they have no clue about, that's because they don't read the most explosive book in the world and they have not accepted the Truths the author of that book gives, or the benefits to life this book has. The book is the Holy Words of God and it is all Truths, the benefits are all encompassing by His only begotten Son Jesus, His word is True, His guidance is Truth, it is all inclusive, what to do and how to act, Let the supreme court make an opposing decision about Gods ordinances and see what happens, oh you can see it, it is reality

Aug 31st Today is the first day of the rest of your life, start it with Jesus, start it with Jesus on your mind, start it with a prayer to our Father through His Son, you see Gods family is all inclusive, the three are in agreement, the Father, the Son, and the Holy Spirit, They are waiting on you, They are waiting on your decision, decide on the Trinity this morning, don't decide on yourself, or any man, before you

decide on the most important relationship of this lifetime and the rest of your life

Aug 30th Where has morality gone, with out Jesus Christ there is none, with out a Savior man is evil, mans agenda is self rightous and self fulfilling, it has nothing to do with love, Jesus has everything to do with love, seek out Jesus He is not hard to find, He has already sought you out He is just waiting for you to recognize Him. Jesus Christ has already paved a Way, we just have to except His Way not our own way, His leads to glory, ours leads to damnation. Jesus is the only Way

Aug 29th Where to begin,begin with Jesus, begin with prayer. God did not ask His only begotten Son to endure what He did for man to deny He existed, what the Father says the Son says and what the Son says the Father says, there is no division, the Son says no one goes to the Father except through the Son, insure God our Father who is in Heaven hears your prayers, accept the Son, Jesus Christ, and the Father will accept you and hear your prayers. Jesus loves you , God loves you, they have both given you a Way to return to them and begin life anew, a life of love not hate, a life of Truth not a lie, find your Way back to the Father through the Son

Aug 28th There is a rainbow in the future, there is an end to all the flooding, there are many floods in our lifes but a mighty God with a mighty right arm will see you through this life and beyond, someone sits on the right hand of the throne of God, it is his Son Jesus Christ, He stopped a flood of Death for those that have accepted His free gift of Salvation, Jesus vis active in believers life's, sometime He is sitting to the Right of our Father who art in Heaven,

God Made You

Introduction and Testimonies

My name is Phillip Scott Davis and I was inspired one day to write a little inspirational post on my beautiful wife Leilani's Facebook. That post grew into many post as she said, if you save just one for Jesus, so I continue. This is really the end of my story. The beginning was when Jesus knocked and I opened the door to a life of blessings. I know now that I am dedicated to Him, and His Father, and the Holy Spirit. In the beginning, I knew Him as a friend who seemed to be by my side always, keeping me from losing sight of Him. He stayed with me were ever I went. I said to myself who is this, and that day when I was 24 He revealed himself to me. I know now that he is my Savior and King, I know now that He is the only begotten Son of God, I know now that he has given me a part of Himself in the Holy Spirit that comforts me. As I started to put together the inspirational I had written on Facebook I noticed that initial one liners were quickly transformed into complete thoughts, however the time spent with God is wonderful and revealing.

I was still lonely and He sent me another my wife, and all of us have continued this march to the throne which is in Heaven. He has sent me to wars and I witnessed what the world is capable of. I found that people that do not know Him do as they please, and in the end their actions turn to violence. Between wars I was at home with my wife and decided to go to bed, while she did not and continued watching T.V. As I started to close my eyes a feeling of pure evil came upon me, the adversary was there. I went in to suggest that my wife come to bed, which she said she would after the show she was watching was over, I returned to bed. Guess what the adversary is persistent, Satan and the evil that flows out of Him had not gone anywhere. My mind reeled as I sought the answer that would drive Him from my home. I slipped to the side of my bed, on my knees, and began praying. As I was praying Jesus clearly said to me, who do you want to handle this, me or your wife, and the adversary fled. My wife is my help mate and helped Jesus reveal himself, He uses all of creation to reveal His truths, all we need do is open our spirits to Him and not the world.

When all my wars were, over I settled in to life here in the community I live in and learned that Jesus was advancing his truth and the realities of a life of service to Him. He sent me to others and told me do what I ask and the rest He would provide, insuring me that he does not task anyone without providing a means to accomplish it. So, I serve Him and those He puts in my path. It is not about who is serving you, it is about who you are serving. Jesus said he will return, so I serve Him with the Talents he entrusted me with, insuring I am advancing His cause and witnessing of the Gospel He has given.

In closing I want to dedicate these inspirational thoughts to Jesus my King, Leilani my wife, and my Church whom Jesus is the Head of sometimes He is standing, but always loving, He has sent His Spirit so we can also love, that includes the unlovable

Aug 27th There is no one more magnifacent than God, all knowing, all seeing, all present, yet so many can not see Him or know His grace. So many people believe the lies of man, but flock to see Gods majisty on display such as the eclipse, and not believe, the wonders of the world are all His, but so many deny Him credit, why are they so blind, so many choose this over the reality of one true God and one true Son of God, God has proven Himself and Jesus has proven Himself,They both said there will be gnashing of teeth in the end, so many throw eternity away, don't let satan ruin your eternity with God

Aug 26th God gives warnings, warnings that are seen and heard way before an event happens. We need to only open our eyes and ears to His very audible voice, you do not see because you choose not to see, you do not hear because you choose not to hear, you can not use any scense you possess unless you open your heart to the cry of our Lord and Savior first. The warnings are given, they are not heeded because your heart is not listening, there are many visual and audible warnings and our response should be be prayer to our Creator through His Son Jesus Christ, you can not serve two masters, your choose is to serve mammon or to serve God, my choose is God

Aug 25th God has given man knowledge, knowledge that man shares with each other to help each other, this knowledge is good, when man perverses this knowledge man has made it evil, all knowledge is good it is man that perverses it, and twist it, and turns it, and uses it for a wrong intention. satan decieves and assist men in changing light to dark, satan does not create he distorts, and man believes a lie, and then begins to replace the Truth with a lie, history is distorted to support lies and the devils agenda. There is a Savior given by our Creator, a Savior that is all Truth, His name is Jesus Christ and when you discover His love your eyes will be opened to the ruses of satan, you will begin to see through Jesus's eyes and realize the manipulation of this world, remember everything was good in the beginning, man has perversed the Truth

Aug 24th Jesus said give to ceasar what is ceasers, people don't understand that there is more to life than the world, If that is all you have then that is all you will receive. Truthfully ceaser did not create you, the world did not create you, God created you and He created you perfect. If you were created perfect where did the inperfection come from, it came from outside influences, it came from satan, it came from other men, it came from ourselfs. There is a Way back to perfection, that Way is thru the Creators Son Jesus Christ, yes you can be perfect again, believe in our Lord and Savior, accept our Lord and Savior, Jesus provides the solution and perfection comes thru Him, be perfected today thru Jesus, be perfect for eternity

Aug 23rd So much is happening in our country, so much is happening in the world, stop and focus, look through all this hate to pure love, a love that does not question, a love that only acts. Let me tell you where you could have witnessed this kind of love, it was on a cross at calvary. Jesus did not ask if He was loved when He was crucified for a hate filled world of sinners, He only acted out of love, you have heard of blind hate, blind rage, will this is blind love, accept Jesus Christ as your Lord and Savior, accept this gift of love He has provided for you

Aug 22nd Everyone watched but how many knew, what happened yesterday was not from a big bang, it did not evolve, it was created, it was created by a all knowing, all seeing, all inclusive God, a God that is singular, there are no others. A man looks at a tree and worships it, the tree was created, a man looks at a rock and worships it, the rock was created, a man looks at the created and makes the created God. There is only one God and He is a jealous God, God did not create for the created to be worshiped, He created so His existance would be known, God created one way out of sin and that is through His only begotten Son Jesus Christ, if you know the Son you will know the Father

Aug 21st Realize what the driving factor of all the hatred in the world is, it is a lack of Jesus Christ, Jesus secured a Way to peace when He died for our sins on a cross, in doing this He provided a Way back into a relationship with our Creator, the one true living God. The world has many false gods that mankind flees to because they lack knowledge of the only Way, the only Truth, and the only Life, with out Jesus man is lost and to satisfy that loss, because they are lost, they attempt to fill a void that only a relationship with Jesus can fill, and they search and search and search, never once lifting the bible and discovering Truth, so they live the only truth they know, a lie, given by the father of lies, there is no truth in him

Aug 20th God does not wonder why, He knows why, He knows that most will not hear Him calling. His voice is only audible to those that listen, initially His calling is faint but listen, to discover Him open your eyes and listen closely, don't focus on a point, open your eyes to all of creation, and see what our Father has created, know that

God Made You

He exist, now that you know of His existance, listen for His calling. Gods call brings you to His only begotten Son, Jesus, if you want a relationship with God you must start with a relationship with His Son, glorify the Son, and you will glorify the Father, grace will shower own on you and your faith in the Trinity of the Father, the Son, and the Holy Spirit, they will flourish others around you and through you

Aug 19th Why don't people attribute creation to our creator, oh they have found giant bones, they must be alien, they can not read the truth that the living word of God proclaims, man tries to make a show of the spiritual world not knowing the consequences for there actions, they refuse to hear the truth that the bible proclaims, nothing is because of our God, it is all about man and what he falsly proclaims to be fact. God hides nothing from His children, Jesus proclaims with a trump that He is Lord an d Savior. So many choose fiction and are in direct opposition to the word of God, do not follow man, follow our King Jesus Christ and succeed in eternity, with out Him you will die the second death

Aug 18th There is only one truth, it seems as everywhere you look all you see is people running full bore with a lie, understand where a lie will take you, closer and closer to the father of lies, people believe lies to be truths when all it takes is a little time to find out the truth. If you read the living word of God you would know Truth and the Truth has set you free if you know Him. Decernment comes with a relationship with Jesus and His Spirit will help you walk with wisdom, our Fatrher in Heaven does not leave us ignorant, He provides all that is needed to know the real answers, yet people do not know because they choose not to, if you are for Jesus be for Him 100% not only when you need Him to put the ball in your court

Aug 17th Jesus said He would make us fishers of men, He said let the chaff grow with the wheat, In the end it will all be seperated. Many men separate themselvesby refusing to believe in a free gift given to them for their transgressions, man thinks they are capable of paying a debt through their own actions, the bible clearly says that Jesus paid a debt for us we could not pay, our very nature will not allow it. Jesus paid that price, in accepting Him your sins are forgivin, your debt is paid, you see God no longer sees you, but sees His Son through you, so quit trying to do something you can never do and accept your Savior and your Lord Jesus Christ, the one that died for you and now lives for you

Aug 16th Saul sought out the people involved in the Way, one day Saul found out that the Way is the onlydirection to move. People will realize that following man will only lead to a second death. Jesus is the Way, follow Him and you will also live in eternity with Him. People will realize that Jesus was sent to earth to redeem those that seek a renewed relationship with our Father who is in Heaven, Jesus is the path that takes us there, He is the only path, He is the only one that has traveled it, without His personal touch our Creator is not attainable, If you deny Jesus God will deny you

Aug 15th So many different groups of people who have nothing in common, they have no idea where they are coming from nor do they know where they are going,they are puppets to the dark powers in high places, this is nothing new, it has already been told of in the living word of God, He said there is nothing new under the sun, that's why in the end there will be a new Heaven and a new earth and the stars will fall from the sky, God will be the light of the world, Jesus Christ is the light of the world now and so many are decieved into believing He is not real, well He is real and reality will reveal itself in the clouds one day, that day do not be one that says I should have believed, every knee shall bow and every tongue confess that Jesus Christ is Lord, that day everyone will have something in common, everyone will see the Truth

Aug 14th A lot of people are not interested in the future or the past, their only interest is now and the only person they are interested in is themselves, and they call us religious zealots if we even attempt to tell them the truth. The truth hurts, everyone that sees creation knows there is a creator, but they choice to believe the lie He does not care, the reality being that He does care and love all of His creation, they choice to believe what they do does not matter, when everything they do is seen by the Creator, and still His love does not diminish for you. Our God gave us a Savior in the form of His only begotten Son Jesus Christ, and while we were still sinners He gave His life up for you, He that had no sin became sin to pay a price we can not pay, and so it is through the Son that we are once again able to reach the Father, the only living God and Creator, let not the devil deceive you anymore

Aug 13th Things that happen in this world and even in our country are not orchestrated by God, man orchestrates his own demise. Open your eyes to the world and all that you will understand is from this world, open your heart to Jesus Christ and you will start to understand this world ,both physically and spiritually. Understand that there is a prince of persia, there is a prince of greece, and there is a prince of the united states, all these princepalities are of satan. Jesus Christ will deliver you from this world and the spiritual world that is all around us, influencing those that belong to the world. Jesus said that if I am for you who can be against you, His words are not fiction, they are truth, He loves you with a love that is not of this world, it is everlasting and complete. The words of God say you can not serve two kinge, either you will hate the one and love the other or you will love the one and hate the other, accept Jesus and you will be refreshed and begin to see the Truth

Aug 12th Who, what, when, where ,and why, the who is Jesus Christ our Lord and Savior, the what is the only begotten Son of God, the when is a little over a thousand years ago on a hill called calvery, the why, which is the reason, Jesus Christ was a sin free Sacrifice for a world of sinners, a perfect sacrifice which made it possible for a sinful and dieing world to be redeemed back to our Father who is in Heaven, Jesus Christ accomplished what no other could, He provided a gift from Heaven that is totally free, a gift of salvation and grace, Jesus said ask and you will receive, He also said you ask not so you have not. Jesus Christ has many names and one is friend, a friend that laid down His life for you, conquered death for all of us, and returned to His loving Father and sat down on a thrown beside our Father. Claim this gift, claim it now, know your Lord and Savior Jesus Christ

Aug 11th Start with a prayer to our Creator through His Son Jesus Christ First thing this morning, and yes it is ok to talk with Him during your first cup of coffee, after all He created it. God wants to have this conversation, Jesus waits for you to arise and begin this prayer, they both long to help, Jesus said give your burdens to me and He said mine are light, in other words don't carry them by yourself, let alone keep them weighing you down. For all this to happen you must have faith, begin your morning with Them, start with We instead of I

Aug 10th There will be some bad times before the return of our Lord and Savior Jesus Christ, many people try to declare that His return is today, tommorrow, or when ever,many people say that this event signals His return, or that event is the time. Jesus said that no one knows but the Father, this is Truth, Jesus said that there will be signs, this is True, Jesus also said many will come claiming that they are Him, and that there will be false prophets, the point is this if Jesus didn't say it, it is not true, He said when He returns everyone will see it, abide in Him and He will abide in you, Truth lies in the relationship of belief and love with Jesus, your eyes are opened, and all doubt is cast aside, you don't have to guess, be assured, accept Jesus Christ as your Lord and Savior and find peace not despair

Aug 9th Open your eyes and your heart to the wonderful grace given to you from our creator, our one true living God. The illusions of a majician leaves you wondering yet the reality of creation you over look, and say there is no God. A diamond is beautiful, but the One that created it is not even noticed, open your eyes to the Creator, the One who has provided a Son to free you from the illusions of this world, a Way to return to Him, a Way to open your eyes to reality, and yes Jesus said I am the Way, no one goes to the Father but through the Son, The Truth, the Truth that will set you free, and the Life, reality not an illusion to keep your eyes distracted from the love of the Father and the Son

God Made You

Aug 8th Isn't it great that because of the love of God and His Son Jesus they have not given up on us, isn't it great that while we really don"t have a plan for eternity that our Lord and Redeemer has already initiated a plan of salvation that brings us back into the loving graces of our Father who is in Heaven, bleesings come from the Father and a single gift of redemption came through His Son Jesus Christ freely given for you to choose, understand that Jesus is at the door knocking, you have to open that door

Aug 7th Do you have a direction in life or do you just go day to day accepting what ever comes your way, if you are you are lost and do not even know it. Satan would want you to believe that there is no hope, and yet when the end comes he will want you to believe he is god, why would he want you to deny the True God and then decieve you into thinking that he is god. Jesus said there will be signs of His return, He tells us how He will return and that the whole world will see His return. Jesus does not try to decieve, He is all Truth. Believe in Jesus and you eill be saved, you will no longer be lost from day to day, satans trinity will be false, Gods Trinity will be True, read the living word of God and understand why your relationship to His Son is so vital to your Salvation, Gods Trinity exist now,quiet your heart and listen for His voice

Aug 6th Who says good morning first, God or you, who says good morning first, Jesus or you, who says good morning first the Holy Spirit or you. You will never say good morning first, God is the Alpha and Omega, the Beginning and the End, Jesus is the Good Shepard, He leads you to green pastures, the Holy Spirit prays for you when you can not pray for yourself. God, His Son, and His Spirit watch over you from eternity till eternity, never stopping, always waiting for you, Jesus said ask and you shall receive, as your walk with Jesus continues you will hear His voice and know Him, His Father, and His Spirit, they will comfort you even in your sleep

Aug 5th Looking for direction, trying to figure out what you are going to do today, start with prayer, do not miss the oppurtunity to serve our risen Lord and Savior today. He needs nothing so when you do serve Him you are serving your neighbor, the one that is lost in depression, the one that sits alone with the blinds pulled down, show them a part of the kingdom of God, tell them of Jesus, of the hope, grace, and fellowship, take time to help them, serve them as Jesus served us, freeing us from the world of non truths and lies, lies that the father of lies uses to decieve and blind those that cannot see hope, there is hope, that hope comes in the form of a Shepard that leads us to green pastures, beside still waters, security in troubled waters, believe in the one that hung on a cross for you, and now lives on the right side of our Creator, believe in Jesus Christ

Aug 4thThere is a problem with man, man wants to make the decisions, not just once in awhile but all the time. Man is not qualified to make any decision alone. Without the knowledge of our creation how can anyone be capable of making a decision, the world attest to the existance of God, creation proves His existance, this is wisdom you can have, there is a problem, you will never acknowledge this wisdom without belief in His Son Jesus, the reason is simple, no one goes to the Father without going through His Son, without His Son you will never obtain wisdom. The wonderful thing is once you accept Gods Son, Jesus

Christ, all the rest comes free through Grace, all keys to eternity are provided, the Father, Son, and Holy Ghost

Aug 3rd Gossip will kill fellowship, murmurs will stop movement, misunderstanding will end a friendship. There is a best selling book that has no misunderstandings, no gossip, and only uses the word murmurs to explain a truth, that book is the living words of the ONE TRUE LIVING GOD, it is the bibles, it holds all answers, most do not want to hear the truth and try to discount it as fiction, it is fact, it holds the Way, the Truth, and the Life, it introduces you to thr Redeemer, a Savior, and a King, His name is Jesus Christ and He is the only begotten Son of God, to know Him is to know salvation

Aug 2ndDecision are made everyday by people that have been to schools of higher learning, and because of that guidance they make the assumption they are correct, they are not. Without seeking the guidance of our Creator all the schooling in this world is for not, people have the knowledge of this world and lack the wisdom of our Lord and Savior Jesus Christ, or our Father who is in Heaven, seek that wisdom through prayer, don't pray with an haughty attitude but one of humility and reverence, have patients and continue in a prayerful attitude, your King will answer, He has promised this, He is all truth

Aug 1st How do so many people feel lost, a Comforter has been provided. How do so many people feel alone, a Guide has been provided. Why are so many people afraid, our Redeemer has walked every road and knows every turn, so turn your eyes to Jesus and He will help you carry your fears, He will walk with you so you are never by yourself, and He will Hold you up as you walk through life. He provides Himself in the Holy Spirit and if He is for you who can be against you. Jesus is the Way, He will provide you with all your needs, and He will intercede for you always with His Father who art in Heaven, choose Jesus and you can not lose, you will be forgiven and will be in Paradise with Him

July 31st God lets people decide on there own fates, many times man does things which are contrary to the Way of God , this is mans plan, a plan with out guidance or direction, and in most cases wrong. If you pray God will give guidance that will direct you toward His love not away from it, if you do it your way you may be walking in the wilderness for 40 years or so, as a matter of fact forever if you don't know our risen Savior and Lord Jesus Christ, Jesus intercedes for us, and He insures our prayers are delivered to our God, Jesus said ask and you will receive. God, Jesus , and the Holy Spirit are in agreement, you need to be in agreement with them, when that happens grace abounds, and blessings are beyond measure

July 30th We have a soveriegn Lord, there is nothing called de javu, there is nothing called karma, there is nothing new under the sun. Our God is the only God, any other is made up by man's imagination, God has written down His word in His book which is the bible, anything other than His word is the word of man, which is a lie, one man does not add to or take away from, as a matter of fact God said anyone
(man or angel) that adds to or takes away from His word is accursed, one man does not decide what the word of God says, we are given a teacher in the Holy Ghost for discernment, you are not alone Jesus Christ who is always true to His word has sent a Comforter, Teacher, Guide, and

He said where two or more are gathered He Himself is there, if God is for you who can be against you

July 29th Someone might hate you if you tell them the truth, is that the problem. People want to stay blind to wrong directions they choose in life, people choose not to tell the truth because they do not want to offend or even worse look the other way when they know the truth. Let me tell you of a Man who died and went to heaven, He died because of your chooses, He died because you chose to look the other way instead of offending someone, He died so the Truth would become a part of your life, He died for nothing He did, He died for everything you did, He died for your sins and transgressions, so choose to look the other way and offend Him, He will forgive you. That mans name is Jesus Christ and He sits at the right Hand of the Father who art in Heaven, He intercedes because you are not capable, He saves your life because you cant, He will tell the Truth, He will not look the other way, He is the Light

July 28th The bible says there is nothing new under the sun, isnt it astonishing that God still loves you, He knows everything there is to know about you and He still wants you. God does not only forgive sin, He forgets it, He forgets it as far as the east is from the west. In His eyes , when you return to Him it is as if you had never left, through His only begotten Son Jesus Christ you are renewed and redeemed, you are a new person, He promises us a new body when He returns to those that belong to Him, but when you accept Jesus as your Savior and Lord you begin a refreshing new life with the Way, the Truth, and the Life, Jesus prepares us to reunite with our Heavenly Father, everything begins anew through Him

God Made You

July 27th What is time to a God that is the Beginning and the End, the Alpna and Omega, yet he understands that , and cares that we can not see eternity yet. He gives so many answers and bleesings on a timeline we can see, but His bleesings continue, there is no end to there beginning, bleesings are for ever and are also a sign of our Divine Creator. His Son Jesus Christ is a sign of our Divine Creator, Jesus is a bleesing from God and so many are blind to Him and His existance, open your eyes and let the Light of the world reveal His Grace and Love, open your eyes and let God reveal His Son to you

July 26th If you are looking for rest give your burdens to Jesus, understand and believe your relationship with the Son of the only true and living God, the Alpha and Omega. Believe that reality rest with Jesus Christ and that He will show you the Way, He is the Light, He is the Good Shepard, let Jesus lead you and guide you, without Him you are lost and will remain lost to the real love that will encompass you within and without, expect the glow that Mose's received when He saw God pass, a glow that can not be exstinguished through time because it is an all consuming love, Jeus has this love for you and always will, this Truth is wonderful and fullfilling, He is with us for eternity

July 25th Open your eyes and look at the many bleesings you receive through out the day. First you woke up to a beautiful world full of our Gods creations, you breathed His grace and joy all day, everything you saw , everything you did was His creation, created for you, a bleesing that last a lifetime. Man did not create anything, satan did not create anything, the only creator is our Father who art in Heaven, He created a Son to show His love and grace to you, while you were still enemies of God He sent His only begotten Son to redeem you, to die for you, to take on all your sins and conquered death for you, through love and grace you were redeemed, through love and faith accept this gift given to you from God through the actions of His Son Jesus Christ

July 24th There is a way, it is not always the easiest way, there may be obstacles in the way, but never the less there is always a way. A way out of trouble that may not be the most convenant, there are no choices in the right way, Jesus said He would provide a way, it is the correct way, it is the only way , it is the direct way, Jesus said I am the way, there is no other way to the Father of creation, the one true God, the only God, and Jesus provides it, no one goes to the Father but through the Son, He is the Way, the Truth, and the Life

July 23rd The Truth is Jesus Christ, the mimic is satan. Jesus is Light He is not capable of lies, satan can disguise himself as an angel of light he is the father of lies. Jesus came to save us, satan only decieves us the truth is not in him. Jesus is the Holy One, satan is the unholy one. Opposites, yet so many are lost, decieved, lied to, oblivious to the evil they serve, Jesus said Father forgive them, they know not what they do, and they don't, we as followers of a risen Lord and Savior must boldly announce the Gospel of Jesus Christ, at least give the lost a chance

July 22nd What drives this venue against our Creator, its not hollywood that is just a tool, what drives this hatred for my Savior Jesus Christ it is not public schools it is just a tool, why the deniel of His Holy Ghost, its not political correctness, a tool also. These are all tools to principalities who are tools of satan, his war is lost and he knows it, to carry as many of the Creators creations to the bottomless pit is his only desire, it is all he has. Stand up for your God, stand up for your Savior Jesus Christ, stand up with the Holy Spirit, share the Gospel of Jesus Christ and deny satan any victories

July 21st Please do not leave our Creator out of your life, everywhere you look something is going on, someone is saying or doing something, but they do not include God or Jesus. Your Savior is real, He is not someone to praise one day a week and forget His existance the other six, if this is the case you do not love Him. Include our Lord and Savior Jesus Christ in all you do and you will find a love not matched here in this world, a Friend who is with you always, Someone who not only shares your burdens but gladly carries those burdens for you, His Spirit will teach you Truths that you could not see with the scales of the world over your eyes, invite Jesus into your life and you will forever be changed into the person of beauty the world would not let you see. Praise God through His Son Jesus Christ

July 20th What are people looking for in life, do they even think of life beyond here or do they even believe in life after death. We did not come from a tadpole or big bang, we were created by the one and only God, the Father of our Redeemer Jesus Christ. man is full of lies and some belong to the father of lies, man did not discover the truth, the Truth introduced Himself in 1st A.D. , His name is Jesus Christ sent from a loving Father in Heaven and they will both be present when all changes to a New Heaven and a New Earth, remember all will meet the Creator and life will contiue with Him or without Him, Jesus is knocking

July 19ᵗʰ Before making a mistake, try praying about what you are about to do or even say. Remember the phrase what would Jesus do, well pray, Jesus said ask and you shall receive, that's praying and that's Jesus answering, His answer will come and you will be enlightened with His wisdom, Jesus loves us and sometimes prayers are not answered as we expect them to be, however His love answers your prayer for the best outcome, not your outcome. Believe in Him and He will lead you to eternity, He has walked through the valley of the shadow of death, He knows the way, if Jesus is for you, and He is, who can be against you

July 18ᵗʰ Everything in the Bible is talked about in a modern public classroom, in the negative, if we do not teach others of the cross which Jesus bore, they will be taught that He did not exist and if He did He was only a man. We must tell the truth to set the captives of this world free, we must tell of Him because He is the Way, Truth, and Life, no one goes to the Father but through the Son. Jesus is the only way to salvation, Jesus asked His Father if there was another way and found that He was the Way. It is up to every individual to open the door that Jesus is knocking at and invite Him into their heart, nothing is forced upon anyone it is freely givin to those that except Him as King and Savior, we must tell of Him

July 17ᵗʰ Look at the world and deny that there is evil in the heart of man, this is because we have been away from the Creator, the One True God, that we have forgotten good, we have forgotten love. There is a way back and that is through our Lord, Savior, and King Jesus Christ, through Him the original sin is forgiven and forgotten, through Him all sin is forgivin and forgotten, He is the Way, the

Truth, and the Life, He holds the key to eternal love. Most are lost, some are searching, and Christians are found, not just a name, a Way of Life with the Father, Son, and Holy Spirit, They guide us, lead us, and most of all Love us, They will not forsake us, all this is Truth

July 16th Christian don't step to the side because someone says they are offended, Jesus said if you deny me, I will deny you. The enemy has his pawns who readily step forward and state they are offended by the words and actions of Christianity, they deny a religion that is not even a religion but a relationship, these other so called religions and gods have no life in them other than the created woshiping the created, As Christians we worship the Creator not the created, we worship through the Creators Son, Jesus Christ, who the Creator sent to pay for the sins of all those that except Him, Christianity is about love from the Father who art in Heaven, and the Son who art in Heaven, and the Holy Spirit who resides in us and prays for us when we cannot

July 15th Think about some of the sayings of man, one in particular, is the grass greener on the other side of the fence. If you follow the Good Shepard you will always find that the grass is greener, He will lead you through an open gate, there is no deception it is all true because He is the Truth. Follow Jesus Christ and all will be provided, sometime some of your wants but always all of your needs, He leads us to His Father, the one and only true God, One that through His love you will long to serve, He will become your want, and your need, you will long to praise His Holy name, just as the seraphims that cry Holy, Holy, Holy!!!

July 14th It escapes me as to why so many are lost, there is a book which is the living word of God, it is called the Holy Bible, it is a guide back to the beginning, back to a relationship with our Creator, there is nothing to add or subtract from what it tells you, a tutor is provided in the Holy Spirit which dwells with you once you begin to understand the why our Savior and Lord Jesus Christ did all He did for us to regain that relationship with the Trinity. Nothing is hidden and it is all truths, open your heart to Jesus and your eyes will be opened to the true nature of our being

July 13th Is anyone interested in the future, or are they just concerned with now. There are consequences to actions and they are called reactions. There is only one way to have bad actions erased and that is to have someone else resolve those actions, resolution from bad actions or sin is given through our Lord and Savior Jesus Christ, man does not forget they maintain a written record, when you are forgivin through Jesus all is erased as if it had never happened, it is forgotten and cannot be found again, it is as far as the east is from the west. Sin is forgiven through the past actions of Jesus, our Savior, our King, His past actions has paid for our future actions if only we ask it of Him, through Him, God forgives and forgets

July 12th Things get rough sometime and sometime it is one thing after another, but look beyond difficulties and look at the beauty behind the scenes. The enemy will deceive you with all the little things that happen and his attempt is to take your focus from our One True God. Without the Holy Spirit residing in you it is with ease he accomplishes this task, but with the gift of the Holy Spirit which comes with your acceptance of Jesus Christ the devils rues are for nought. Rely on God, rely on Jesus, rely on the Holy Spirit and burdens seem to fade away as you think of the glory of the Trinity

July 11th I can only tell you of the love that your Creator, Jehovah, The One True God has for you. I can only tell you of the Love that Jesus, The only begotten Son of God has for you. I can only tell you how to receive the grace of our Savior, King and Redeemer. I can only tell you of how He became 100 % man and 100% God to live the life that you now live without sin and died to pay a price for our transgressions, paid in full to our Father who art in Heaven, I can only tell you of all these wonderful gifts including the Holy Spirit to help in your restoration. It is your choice, that is something I cannot do for you, decide, eternity is the only thing at stake, besides your soul

July 10th Is it to hard to change, are you afraid to give up material items, don't you believe that there is more and more abundance to have, or are you satisfied with the zig-zag path this world offers. This world offers only one thing, eternity with the father of lies. Turn your eyes toward Jesus, He promises truth, He promises life abundant, He promises a relationship with our Father which art in Heaven, He promises you an eternity of Glory, and so so much more that the earth could not hold the volumes of books if it was all told, don't listen to the lies of this world, listen to the truths of Jesus Christ, don't accept temporary, accept permanant from Jesus the only begotten Son of God, our Savior and King, His burden is light, the world will drag you down

July 9th Do people feel that since it is free it is not worth it, the greatest gift that a person can receive is free, yet people don't want it because it is free. Jesus wants you to come to

Him as you are, you do not have to clean up to be accepted by Him, He said He will clothe you, as a matter of fact the very instance you accept Him He begins to set you free from the filth of this world. Don't just accept what this world has to offer when an eternity of joy and rest is knocking, waiting for you to open up, cleansing begins with Jesus Christ and life never ends with Jesus Christ

July 8th Isn't it wonderful that God has put His signature out in the open so no one can say I didn't know. So many people try to deny that a creator exist, they cannot because as Jesus said the very rocks will cry out. Our Father did not create rocks to praise Him, He created you to praise Him, He created you for fellowship, cry out to your Heavenly Father and He will provide in over abundance, but you cannot even approach with out going through the door, Jesus Christ is that door, He is the way, the only way, our works will not move the curtain to the Holie of Holies, only the strength of Jesus, He is the Truth, and the Life

July 7th Why does the world impose itself on the church which Jesus Christ is the Head, islam does not have this problem, buhhda does not have this problem, nor any other, only christianity , why. Non of the others have guidance from a risen Savior. The world is attempting change the living word of God by hiding it behind political correctness, behind the stigma of hate, behind any deception possible to prevent the spread of the truth, the Gospel of Jesus Christ, Christ gave all so that all may live, this Gospel is for everyone, the problem is it is not accepted by everyone, proof is in creation, proof is in the only begotten Son of the Creator, our Heavenly Father

July 6th Know that Christianity is under attack, an attack administered by people that have no understanding about this world and who rules it, they have no belief in things unseen and are easily manipulated by the father of lies. The truth is not in them because they do not know the truth, it is easy for them to do as they please because they have never been subjected to the truth nor care to know it, share the Gospel of Jesus Christ and help our King and Savior to let these captives of satan free, all will not accept the Truth, but some will come to know our Redeemer, pray for those that are lost. God has a plan for those that accept His only begotten Son, and He has a plan for those that don't

July 5th The world that our creator created is full of wonders and marvels, but don't lose focus on the one He created for your salvation, nothing of this world can claim the grace Jesus Christ gives us. As you explore this world don't try to do it on your own, upon accepting Jesus you are also given a guide in the Holy Spirit. You can not rely on your own instincts or that of a friends, you only have the knowledge of what you know, there is so much more to this creation that you don't know, so rely on Jesus and He will guide you in love, others do not possess the knowledge to take you through the valley of death, as danger approaches He will warn you and protect you, some things He is the only one that can, oh what a friend we have in Jesus

July 4th Today is a holiday, voted in by politicians, give to ceaser what is ceaser's. It is independence day, let me tell you of another day that is also a holyday, the day Jesus Christ gave all of us independence from this world, and gave us another, full of words like grace, faith, redemption, pardon, freely given, a burden that is light,and many, many more words that are only associated with the love of our

Creator, our God, has for what He has created, accept the full pardon of Jesus, He accomplished all that is required and freely gives that pardon to you

July 3rd Free samples are everywhere and everyone flocks to get their freebie, some people say that nothing is really free, I say there is something completely free. God has provided a way to return to Him through His only begotten Son, this free item is new, nobody else can receive this item, it is only yours and it waits for you to accept it, but everyone is not running to redeem it, most do not even know about it. It insures that you are part of redemption from this world, it insures that you are saved from a death sentence, it will never harm you, what is this free gift, it's a gift from our Creator, through His Son, to you. This gift comes in many names, but has one purpose, to save you from an eternity of loneliness. Redeemer, Savior, Lord, King, The Way, Jesus Christ, He paid a price you could not and made a way out of this world of sin, redeem this free gift, and give your burdens away

July 2nd If you don't pray you don't have the right to ask why. Often, we ask why me, but in a lot of cases God is our last resort not our first, make God your first resort. When you do this, you will see the difference in your life, things will begin to have reason and purpose. Some we will not understand, but Gods word says that there is a season for everything, make Jesus Christ your first season, not your last, make Him number one, He is the Beginning and the End, make Him a part of your life not an afterthought, after all He is your King and Savior

July 1st If you can't see it you don't believe in it, open your eyes, if you can't feel it open your heart. Everyone of Gods creations is loved by Him, including you, you are loved just the way you are, open your heart to our Lord and Savior, Jesus Christ, and you will see Him, you will Hear Him, and you will feel Him. He is the only Way. Stop and talk to Him, He will respond, many people are blessed but are blind to it because they don't expect it, think about your life without Jesus Christ and you will find blessings, think about your life with Jesus and you will see many blessings. To be complete reunite with our Creator and His Son, completeness doesn't stop with a wife and children, completeness stops with Jesus Christ, who is given power to complete you

June 30th, You have choices, you can pray or not pray, you can accept Jesus or not, nothing is forced upon you, you do not die because you do or don't, the first death. The second death is the one that there is no turning back from, the last judgement is the final sentence of death, those that have not chosen are going to go to the bottomless pit, separated from God, separated from Jesus, and separated from love, alone forever, Don't wait, choose Jesus Christ, the Way, the Truth, and the Life, no one goes to the Father except through Him, the price He paid on the cross and death is the reason the final Judgment of our Father, Abba, which art in Heaven will condemn those that have chosen to ignore the gift of Salvation His Son Jesus Christ provides

June 29th So many people are lost to the truth of their own existence, not knowing if they come from a pool of slime on the edge of land, or from an alien ship from another planet, so many people are lost and are willing to give away their own soul to belong to something. Jesus Christ wants the truth to be told, the truth of redemption He provided on Calvary, people are lost, people are searching, we must share the Good News, don't hate the lost, love them and lead them to salvation which is provided by Jesus, which is provided by God, which is provided by the Holy Spirit, share the truth

June 28th In the beginning, you had no knowledge of living a life with your true Father who art in Heaven and the father of lies, as you grew God began to draw you toward His Son Jesus. Some have found the true Savior of this world however He said many would come claiming they are the true messiah and not to believe them, yet many were lost and began following false messiah's, and worshipping false idols, the written word will show clearly all that are false, read God's word and obtain a clear vision to see all the false imposters employed by satan. Call on Jesus He is your only ally against spiritual enemies of His Father the one true God, our Father and Creator, Jesus has already prepared the Way because He is the Way

June 27th Let God bless you, so many are waiting on those that choose Him. If you feel blessed without knowing our true Lord and Savior Jesus Christ they will only be temporary, the world cares naught for you, enjoy the true love of Jesus, He said no one goes to the Father except through Me, Jesus wants to bless you, He wants you to prosper, He wants you to succeed, He wants you to return to the Trinity, He wants fellowship with you, He came as a Servant to pay a price you could not, and now He is a loving King who will bring you to His side to reign over nations, He longs to return you to The Great I Am

June 26th Why, why as Christians are we under attack, because Jesus, the only begotten Son of Jehovah our God, is the Way, the Truth, and the Life. Those that don't know this truth are lost and only have the world to turn to, or wonder why you as a Christian have faith in God the Father, Jesus his only begotten Son, and the Holy Ghost that resides in us, not willing to turn from their false idols they persecute the Truth because they are not willing to give up a lie. Look at the news as the idol of islam crept into the belief system of those that are still lost, or budda is portrayed as love, there is only one love and one way to salvation, true love in our Lord and Savior Jesus Christ

June 25th satan never cried out for you, satan never created anything, satan never cared for anyone, everything he tells you is a lie. So many people follow his easy path, he promised nothing, and so many follow him. Jesus said you cannot serve two masters, you will hate the one and love the other or you will love the one and hate the other, Jesus Christ is all truth, He cannot tell a lie. Happiness is the love for Jesus Christ not love of the world. Choose Jesus his burden is light, He cares about you, He will not turn you away, it does not matter how dirty you are, in Him you begin anew, you are reborn, and washed by His blood, all His acts where for your redemption. Make a choice for Jesus Christ the one that gave all for you, or make none and your choice is given to you in the one that truth will never exist in

June 24th What will happen when the King returns, He comes to subdue the nations, but before that He will gather His people to Him, first the dead in Christ, then the living. You don't have to belong to a gang to be accepted, you don't have to be part of a certain group, you must be a part of a family, the family of God. There is no initiation, you simply need to accept Jesus Christ as your personal Savior and Lord, you are already a precious gift in Jesus Christ eyes and He watches you and waits patiently for you to turn and return to Him, you are accepted just the way you are, understand who your Savior is, He is the one that died on golgatha He paid all the price that you owed, your debt is paid and you are free, find Jesus Christ and run to Him, He is not hard to find He is already waiting for you

June 23rd Why worry about life, don't you know that our Heavenly Father is still creating. Look how many flowers a bee must draw nectar from, and yet we worry, He said how much more will He feed you. You sustain your own worry's, but if you look at the promises in God you will find sufficient truths that will vanquish all your worries. Start with Gods only begotten Son, Jesus Christ is the conduit to eternity, He insures all your provisions for this life and your next, accept what is provided by our Creator in His Son Jesus Christ, and you will find happiness beyond measure

June 22nd Don't forget to pray for each other, so many times fellow Christians reach a stopping point and need to be revitalized, the Holy Spirit is praying for them when they cannot pray for them self's, so keep all your prayers inclusive of all you know, Sometimes the prayers that you pray for another individual are equally inclusive of you. Jesus said love your neighbor as yourself, He also said there is no stronger love than to die for a friend, He has already done that for all of us, so pray through our Savior and King to our Heavenly Father and include friends that you do not see pray for each other because we all need fellowship through prayer, and Jesus will carry all your needs to His Father and our Father

June 21st Jesus is always searching for lost souls, souls which are lost in a world full of deceptions and lies. Do not be fooled by those that say I am the messiah, they are not. Study the living word of God to ensure that you are wearing the full armor of God, prepare for the battles you will come across and never forget that once you accept Jesus Christ all your battles are over, He will insure victory in every battle that you come across because He fights for you and He has already conquered all that you can conceive rather physical or spiritual. Rest in your Saviors arms He will not forsake you, He said this and all Jesus Christ says is truth, with Him you are truly redeemed

June 20th What would our Heavenly Father want us to do today, one thing, tell the lost people of this world of His only begotten Son Jesus Christ. People look all over for a champion to aspire to be like, one is provided in our Lord and Redeemer, He will provide you with an eternity of love, love that will lead you through life, one that will protect you from things seen as will as not seen, all creation answers to Him, He has been given all things from His Father, our Creator, with Jesus you cannot go wrong, so share your Lord and Savior with the world, the world cannot hurt Him, it already tried and failed, our enemy who is satan has tried and failed, Jesus is our Champion open the door and let Him in, and if He is already a part of your life, share what He has done for you

June 19th Why do people keep searching for perfection without the realization that all they have to do is look, open your eyes to the perfect One open your eyes to Jesus Christ. After you have done that you will find perfection, God made perfection and perfection came to earth to die for us, to pay a price we could not pay, Jesus came to accomplish something we could never accomplish, and it took perfection to do all that the only begotten Son was willing to do, He died alone so that all of us could love, He said that there is no better love than to die for a friend, and yes you are friend, oh what a friend we have in Jesus

June 18th Aren't you glad that Jesus hasn't decided it isn't worth it, aren't you glad that Jesus never said that you were not worth it. What you really need to do is decide if you are worth it? The world would have you think that there is nothing more but I will tell you there is so much more and it all starts with Jesus Christ, a relationship that you alone have to decide if you are worth, Jesus certainly thinks you are worth it or He would not have endured what He did, all the way to death and back. Jesus Christ is why any of us are worth it, and He continues to knock because He thinks that we are worth every drop of blood He gave to cleanse us, Jesus loves us this I know for the Bible tells me so

June 17th Why don't people believe, it is because it is beyond our understanding. Why should you be saved and nothing beyond belief is required, no works are required to join our God in the New Jerusalem, only faith in His Son Jesus Christ, He is the conduit between our Creator and our self's, without Him you cannot reach eternity, an eternity living in a mansion built by a heavenly carpenter named Jesus Christ, He has gone to prepare a place for you, this is truth, and He will return to take us there, this is truth, it all starts with Jesus and ends in Glory, accept our Savior

June 16th What do people believe, do they believe in evil, or do they believe in good. People search all over the world to find these revelations, all they find in the world are lies perpetrated by the father of lies. There is only one source for the answers people search for and that is the Holy Bible, reading will not garner the answers people search for, the truth will be hidden from their understanding. To understand everything, you must rely on one, that is Jesus Christ, and with Him your eyes will be opened to the truth, all answers will become crystal clear through His strength and His spirit, He is the Life

June 15th, It seems that there is an active agenda to belittle Christianity, the ones that perpetrate this do not know who they are in league with and are blind to the lies they spread, we must ask God to forgive them. However, be aware that Christians are under attack, yes even in the United States. Christians, you need to pray to our Father who art in Heaven through His only begotten Son Jesus Christ for strength to prevail, Jesus said that His strength is yours, He said He will not forsake you, He said He will not leave you, He is Truth, He cannot be defeated and through Him you cannot be defeated. Pray through Jesus Christ He is our Redeemer

June 14th If you want knowledge you can get it in this world, in this world you will obtain knowledge both good and bad. If you want to go a step further and gain understanding of that knowledge, and above knowledge, wisdom, our Heavenly Father has left His living word in the Bible, there is one stipulation, and that is the acceptance of His only begotten Son Jesus Christ, who intern gives you a live-in tutor to the words of His Father in the Holy Ghost. Jesus Christ is the only Way, the only way to begin this journey to eternity in a new Heaven and a new Earth. You are not alone, nor will you ever be once you accept Jesus in your Heart

God Made You

June 13th Do you even care to include your Lord and Savior in your planning, probable not if you do not know Him? Let me introduce you to Him, His name is Jesus Christ and He resided with our Father who art in Heaven, our Creator. Our Father asked His only begotten Son to become like a man to endure all the trials, tribulations, and temptations that would ever befall man, to be beaten by man, spit upon by man, tortured by man, and then die for man and his sins through crucifixion all while the spiritual leaders of man belittled Him while He suffered onto death on a cross, rejected by man and lost from His Father because of our sins. He is alive, He paid a price we could not, He conquered death and was resurrected to His Fathers throne, there Jesus intercedes on our behalf with our God and Creator, so include Him in all your plans and your plans will never fail

June 12th Where are you at this morning, taking care of what the outside looks like, ignoring the inside. It doesn't matter what the outside looks like if the heart is dark. Jesus said I am the Light, he is the only one that can heal your heart. Jesus came to restore us, He doesn't just cover a blemish, He removes it as far as the east is from the west. Jesus is not a makeup you apply from the outside daily, He is love that begins on the inside and restores all including your heart. He is the Way, the Truth, and the Light

June 11th Where is Jesus in your life, is He an afterthought, is He a go to in case of emergencies, just where is Jesus on your list of priorities. Oh your saving the best for last, no you're putting the best last, put Jesus first in your life instead of putting life first, when you do you will begin to find a peace you did not know existed, an existence above life, a meaning for life, what you did before was flirt with the enemy, playing Russian roulette with life, because there was no purpose, give your life a purpose, open the door to a Savior and a King, open the door to Jesus and truly begin to live

June 10th Jesus had nothing to hide from anyone, truly what you see is what you get. His love for you never falters, He will wait forever for you to accept Him, He has already died for you and paid the price of admission to heaven for you. No one on this earth has done or will ever do the things that Jesus has done for you. If anyone denying is done it is through eyes that have never opened. There is no other name given for Salvation, many will try to deceive you and say that they are the Messiah but they are not, do not be fooled by them. Everyone will see Jesus when He returns. Start a relationship with Jesus which will blossom into the truth of our existence and the love the Trinity has for you

June 9th Peace, tranquility, happiness, you might believe you have found it. These things cannot happen without Jesus being present in your life, the places you go to relax may give you a temporary boost. A life with Jesus gives you a permanent boost, one that will last an eternity, anything man does is only here briefly here, a relationship with our creator is always. Start and finish your day with Them in prayer, Jesus Christ said He would never leave you or forsake you, and He won't, Allow Him to give you the light of life and He will also give you a piece of Himself in the Holy Spirit, you will never be alone again

June 8th Don't chase the shiny object on the side of the path, don't be distracted from the truth, follow Jesus Christ and you will not go wrong, satan will entice you with things he knows will pull you in a wrong direction and he will continue until your eyes are no longer on Jesus, you find that all of a sudden you are lost, don't panic, cry out to the one and only begotten Son of God, He will find you. Don't try to find your way alone, you will remain lost forever. Jesus is the way, and He knows the way, so cry out to Him, He will find you and take you back, oh what a love we have in Jesus

June 7th What God has created is perfection, what God has ordained is perfect, yet man wants to judge his decisions. Man is always trying to put a round peg in a square hole, and man will succeed after he has either distorted the peg or the square, and he will call this creation. God created, Jesus created, the Holy Spirit created, man did not create, he is created, Satan has not created, he was created. Satan was the original author of altering perfection, that is why he is going to the bottomless pit. Trust in our Father who art in Heaven, trust in His only begotten Son Jesus, trust in the Holy Spirit, their ways lead to perfection. Trusting in imperfection only leads to one thing imperfection

June 6th Put Jesus on the pedestal He deserves to be on, He is the sole authority on life. Why a man or a woman think they have the rights of our sovereign King reminds us of how many lost souls are in this world. Jesus said I am the Way, there is no other way. He alone holds the keys to Heaven and the bottomless pit, He alone is the determining factor for Eternity, it was finished at the cross, no other works are required and anyone that says that there is a liar and a child of the father of lies. Do not let the world deceive you, Jesus is the plan for Salvation, He is our Savior, accept Him and the only plan for redemption

June 5th Man is not capable of creation without distortion, man cannot take from an already created world and call that creation his. Man is capable of only two things, following the Truth or telling a lie. Man can alter creation but for one reason, that is that the Creator allowed it. Man, only manipulates creation or the proper order of things, the law has already been given by God, to manipulate the law is to perverse creation. Let God prevail in your life and you will begin to understand His creation, don't follow man and the world, they only manipulate the truth, making it a lie. Jesus said am the Truth, accept Him and His Spirit will begin to unravel all the lies, distortions, and perversions of the Enemy, accept Jesus Christ and return to your original estate

June 4th What beautiful blessings come from our Lord, He willingly gives to those of us that are a part of the Kingdom of Heaven. Jesus tells of the blessings that abound for those that are, and they are never ending. Talk with the one and only God, our Father in Heaven, that is how Jesus said address Him. Our God is that personal with those that love Him, He loves us and wants to bless us every second of every day. Oh what a Savior, oh what a King, Oh what a God, all knowing and all loving, don't look past the blessing of Jesus Christ, He waits for us with an undying love

June 3rd Blessings come from God, they are not given by any other persons, everything that exist is because of our Father in Heaven. The greatest blessing is His Son Jesus Christ. Jesus is the beginning of a life of blessings. Ask God through His Son to bless all you do in life, if Jesus is in your life you will begin to notice the very air you breath is a blessing, your eyes will be opened to the things that at one point in your life you thought were just a part of life. Without Jesus you have no life, you are only waiting for death, you have nothing to look forward to, you don't even know in the end you will be in the bottomless pit. I pray all eyes are opened to the wonderful blessing of Jesus Christ

June 2nd Don't believe lies, Jesus said He is the Truth, no one else can claim this title. Jesus said there will be many deceivers that claim that they are the messiah, do not believe them, they lie and are children of the father of lies. If you follow Jesus you will not be deceived He has already for warned you of these things. The Bible tells all truths and has not left us blind to the assailant that denies the truth. Jesus is the Messiah and Lord and Savior and King, He is our sword and Avenger, His love is ever lasting therefore Jesus is everlasting, accept Him now and begin a journey to a mansion in the sky

June 1st It does not matter where you are in life to God, He can and will use you to accomplish glory. Quit trying to second guess the King of Eternity, He knows your flaws and He still loves you with an undying love. You may be a reason for someone else's decision to accept the King of Kings, and Lord of Lords, even if you won't give yourself credit, Jesus will give you all the credentials you will ever need, with God all things are possible, oh how He loves us, won't you find Him, it is not hard, just turn around, He is that close

May 31st Why does our Lord Jesus Christ wait on His Fathers creation to recognize Him, because what He did on a tree in calvary He did for all that are lost. The opportunity to return to Salvation was given freely and is presented to all, because tomorrow your brother, sister, mother, father, or friend might find Jesus. Jesus said love your neighbor as yourself, He wants them to have the same chance at redemption as you, so share the Gospel of Jesus

Christ if it means redemption for one more soul that is lost. Jesus loves all and is knocking on the lost's door even today

May 30th You are alive, and with Jesus you are not searching for a purpose. When you accept Him as Lord and Savior you are filled with purpose, The Holy Spirit brings direction into your life, you begin to live for others and feel a scence of a need to look beyond yourself but toward others, Jesus said love your neighbor as yourself, so you have a want to help, a need to help and share the Gospel of Jesus Christ. Share His name while becoming closer and closer to Him

May 29th Lord help them to see you more clearly, help them to understand your words of love. Jesus Christ is the only divine Savior that all other religions do not have. I wonder why that is, because Jesus Christ, the only begotten Son of God is the only Way, The only Way to what, a relationship with God, Jesus's Father, our Father, our creator. Jesus, like his Father cannot tell a lie, Jesus is the Truth. And without Jesus you have no life, He is Life. Man's religions have none of these, there is no truth in them, therefore they have none of the Divinity in them, Jesus said that many will come with the claim that they are the Messiah, don't believe them

May 28th Wake up with a prayer this morning, a prayer of praise for what the only True God has done for you. Wake up this morning with a prayer on your lips, a prayer thanking Gods only begotten Son Jesus for what He has done for you. Wake up and acknowledge what the Trinity has given you. Insure that you know Jesus, reaffirm your love for Him and soon you will join the chorus of the angels in rejoicing and praise for our Savior and Lord, you will want to because He is deserving of all praise, He died in your place so you could return to the relationship you had with Jesus, His Father who is the Creator of all, and the Holy Spirit, with this restored relationship you are saved

May 27th No matter where you are, Jesus Christ is with you, no matter what you are doing Jesus Christ is beside you, as you go down the wrong path, Jesus Christ is telling you. As you continue walking down the wrong path, Jesus Christ is watching you, waiting for you to turn around, if you do you will see that Jesus Christ is crying for you. He loves you with an undying love. As you grow closer and closer to Him, He grows closer and closer to you. Don't forsake Him for a so-called friend, Jesus is not a so-called friend, Jesus is a friend in deed. Nothing replaces the true love that Jesus Christ has for you, He is waiting with open arms for you to return to Him, and this love man or angel cannot take from you, it is a love that has no end, you are Jesus's true love

May 26th Some explanations of life that some people believe is beyond the scope of human intelligence, we do not evolve into a Christian, those of us that are Christians chose to accept Jesus Christ as our Savior and Lord. We did not evolve, we were created in the image of God and it starts with the creation of a man named adam. A false god would have you believe it started in a vast ocean were amazingly enough cells came together, others a big bang in space, no it was from a God who's name Yahweh and his intelligent design of man and everything else you see or don't see, He also created a Savior for you and I named King of Kings, Lord of Lords, Jesus our only conduit back to our creator and God, accept Him now as your Lord and Savior

May 25th There is plenty of time to wait, only an eternity. Jesus has been waiting on you since the creation of time, day one. One day He will stop knocking as He prepares to return to this world as a King, He will no longer have the separation of anything between you and Him. He said that there will be those that claim to be Him before then, but don't believe them they are false, when Jesus returns every eye shall see Him, there will be no doubt. Quit waiting for tomorrow to commit to our Lord Jesus Christ, there are many that claim to be like Him but they will falter in the Light of Him, there is no substitute, only Jesus holds the keys. Begin to worship Him today, now

May 24th Don't think for a minute that God has planned any of the evil that happens in this world, man can devise evil on his own, out of his own heart. You may wonder does God care, yes God cares, the ones that have only evil in their hearts do not care about God, many have turned their backs on God and Jesus, these people have no good in their souls and have chosen to be children of the devil not knowing or believing the truth, because there is no truth in them. The living word of God has told us that the sun will rise on both the saved and the lost, things will become as in the days of Noah, yes there are signs that tell us, those that are saved can see, the unsaved have no clue. Share the gospel of Jesus Christ and the truth will set them free

May 23rd What do we want, we want it our way, our way is not always the correct way, we can't see what the future holds, it's like the song says sometimes we need to praise God for unanswered prayer. It is not until events unfold that we find what we thought we needed or wanted was best, only to find out that it would have been a detriment. Let's do agree on one thing that Jesus Christ is the way, the truth. and the life, He knows what our needs are and He loves us enough not to give us everything we want. Use prayer as a way of life, prayer through Jesus to our Heavenly Father, they will lead us down the correct paths in life through love

May 22nd The greatest person in this world is looking for you, His name is Jesus. If you know Him you know what He can do, if you don't look to the word of God. The bible contains all truths, it tells of correct ways to live your life. To begin with start a relationship with a Savior and a King, a Redeemer and a Creator, and a God that knows everything about your past, present, and future and still loves you. The beginning is Jesus, the ending is an eternity spent in Heaven, don't seek advice from men who do not know Jesus, they have no direction and will lead you down a path of destruction, Jesus is the foundation for life, and He will lead you down a path of righteousness, please do not be fooled any longer by the ruler of this world, believe in the Alpha and Omega, the Beginning and the End

May 21st So much to absorb, some will just give up and go along with the status quo. Let me tell you if you expect the status you with Jesus Christ you are wrong, all the lies that satan has portrayed and so many have accepted as truth has become the status qou. For your eyes to be opened you need to cry out to Jesus, and He will reveal the truth about the lies that inhabit so much of the world, He will not let you forget the disgraces that man has thrown in the face of His Father. Hard life is hard, so hard that without Jesus Christ as your personal Savior and King, you will not survive as His Father created you to survive, you were created for fellowship with our God. You were created as children of God, don't let the world deceive you into thinking you are children of satan

May 20th This is a new day, a day to begin a new life with the King of eternity, or remain with the lying slum lord of the bottomless pit. Satan wants you to believe that all has already been decided for you and that there is no way out of this rat race we began life in. Well there is way, only one way, begin by affirming that Jesus is the only begotten Son of God, that He came to earth as a man living a life without sin, dying on a cross to redeem you and I, and being resurrected on the third day, returning to the right side of the Fathers throne anointed Savior and King for all that accept Him. Jesus came to save us, to free us from this world so we can once again have the relationship with God we were always supposed to have

May 19th Wake up to what is really going on around you, don't just sit back and watch, be aware. Things that you cannot discerned, things you do not understand, things you may never see until it is too late. Open your eyes to Jesus Christ and He will open your eyes to things seen or not seen, He enables discernment of physical and spiritual events, things which are happening daily, right in front of you. Without the protection of the Holy Spirit you are vulnerable to all the lies and illusions that satan throws your way, things that are not supposed to be, acceptance of acts which contradict the words of God. Give yourself to Jesus and you will see all the things in this world that should not be, He will open your eyes to the true reality around you, He will protect you, and guide you to eternal life with Him

God Made You

May 18th Looking for inspiration this morning, look no further than the biblical truths contained in the bible. Man inspires man to live surrounded by unbiblical truths, Unbiblical truths are nothing more than lies fabricated by the father of lies the devil. You did not evolve into the wonderful creation you are, God created you for perfection, to live with Him, satan wants you to believe you make your own destiny, God has already prepared a destiny for you through His Son Jesus Christ, accept the destiny that was prepared for you by a living God, accept Jesus as the One preordained to prepare this free gift of salvation

May 17th Blessings flow from our Savior and King, He is the King of kings, and no one goes to the Father except through Him. There is so much more to the kingdom of God Jehovah, two of Them being the Son and the Holy Spirit, and the Son holds the keys to forever. This world has an end but the love of Jesus goes on. The kingdom will have a new Heaven and a new Earth all that is old will pass away, accept the free gift of salvation that Jesus Christ provides, become a child of God once more and let the relationship of renewal and love begin flowing like living waters that He alone provides

May 16th do you feel secure, and if so are you really secure? If you have not accepted the Way, the Truth, and the Life you will never be secure, Jesus gives whole body assurance, without Him nothing is finished, Jesus vis the only one that proclaimed it is finished. Some synonyms for finished are over, done, complete. Accept the gift that will never tarnish, accept Jesus Christ, His gift which is free is multi-faceted, you receive Him, His Father, the Holy

Spirit, and an eternity of salvation and love. Insure you are really secure.

May 15th Is there anything new under the sun, nothing new but the discovery of a loving God, one who gave up His only begotten Son to save you. If you don't know Jesus search Him out, it isn't hard because He is waiting for you on the other side of the door. Get to know Him and accept Him for who He is, Savior and Lord, before eternity arrives. That's right eternity begins after this life, you have now to accept the gift of redemption from our Heavenly Father, that gift comes through His Son Jesus Christ, and find a love that is eternal

May 14th Today we honor mothers, God honored mothers also, He chose a virgin mother to bring the joy of Jesus into this world, woman was created to be a helpmate to the first adam and the second Adam, as a matter of fact no other helpmate was found in all of creation to do what a woman and mother could do, so mothers were created last, and it was a mother named mary that was first to hold our Savior Jesus Christ. A mother was chosen to begin Gods redemption plan here in this world. Without a mother in a manger we would not have been able to be saved, but a mother was there and our Heavenly Father was there, and after a miraculous birth our King and Savior came to pay a price we could not pay ourselves. Honor mothers, they play a role in our salvation

May 13th, we forget but God never forgets he sent his only begotten son to remind us of his love anything that we find herself in Temptations or trials he is with us and God knows all our needs God is the great physician his son

Jesus is the great physician rely on them and you will find no relevance and any other love them as I love you

May 12th What are people looking for, security, Jesus said He would never forsake you. Companionship, Jesus said He would never leave you. Protection, Jesus has sent His Spirit to live with in you. All of Jesus's promises are true, they are validated through the love He has for you. With Him there is always a way out of any situation you find yourself in. He is our Savior, He is our King, He is the only begotten Son of God, our Creator who has chosen you just as you are, with all the blemishes of this world, Jesus will wash away the grime of this world and make you a new person, one who has been washed by the blood of the Lamb

May 11th Isn't it refreshing to know that you are a part of the kingdom of God, isn't it wonderful to know that Jesus is your Savior and King, He watches over you always, nothing happens without His knowledge and He will provide a solution to all your problems. Start with prayer today, pray to the Father through His Son Jesus Christ who is always available to you, God is in your support channel, Jesus is in your support channel, and the Holy Spirit is in your Support channel. They are available from the beginning, why wait until despair hits you, go to them as a first resort not a last resort

May 10th Things could have been so much worse, God does watch over you even with all our flaws. We see flaws Jesus sees perfection, He wants you to come to Him now. With Jesus, you have nothing to change, or hide He knows all of you and still loves you. You see we see all of what we call imperfection and ask how, Jesus sees all the perfections and loves you. Go to Him as you are and He will change your life, there are so many great and marvelous things He will show you every day as you walk together. His love is the perfect love and once you open the door to your heart you will find answers you could never see before. So, walk with Him and talk with Him, His revelations are unending

May 9th how can we find happiness, it is provided by a loving Father and Creator. We make decisions which alter the life He has promised. Who we choose, what we choose, when we choose, all these chooses that we decide, His promises are true, start your day in talking with Him, include God and His only begotten Son Jesus Christ in your decision-making process and you will find that things are a whole lot smoother, after they know you best because they knew you before you knew yourself. When you bring the King above all Kings into your life, listen to His advice, He knows the way, He knows the temptations, He knows the obstacles, He is the Way, the Truth, and the Life, He holds the keys to an eternity of happiness.

May 8th Stop before you start today, think of what your actions may lead you into. That's right it is your actions and your decisions that take you to the places you went to, or moved you to the places you are. You don't always make the correct turns, there is some one that has traveled the roads of this world and survived and His name is Jesus, He will insure you traverse this world and come out a winner in the end. This world is going to end for you and me, Jesus has traveled there also and came out victorious and now sits at the right hand of the throne of God, you can trust Jesus because He cares more for you than you care yourself. His love is infinite and will never die, listen to Him and receive eternity

May 7th so, you don't have enough time for the Creator of time, seems kind of ironic doesn't it. He assures you that you have adequate time for everything, if you don't guess who has not planned correctly, surely not the One that created all you see in six days. He has provided you time to worship Him, excuses do not come from Him they come from you. He has provided a Savior for you and He found time to die on a cross for you. God has found time to draw you to His Son so you will have an eternity of time to be with Them. You have the time, you are too busy with that extra hour of sleep, you are too busy with that show that you are watching. You don't have to make time, you have to take time away from nothing, for Jesus who will give you everything

May 6th Don't you understand, all that your Savior has done for you is out of an intense love, He begs for you to just glance His way, a King looking toward His people for recognition. He knows you and everything about you and He still longs for a long-lost relationship with you, it was lost in the Garden of Eden and it began to be restored in the Garden of Gethsemane. If you are lost in this world all you have to do is cry out to Jesus, He will answer you. Don't let the deceiver influence you with the beauty of his lies, Jesus treasures you and you are worth the price He paid for you, if you were not He would not have died for you.

May 5th the Creator knows the needs of the created and God is the Creator of everything seen and unseen, so why rely on the created to determine reality, what will be and not. Man attempts to change the laws that God has ordained, things which God created to work together, and people will ask what is going on, they see nothing of reality because they have been blinded to the truth by the world which by the way is created by God, return to the truth and if you have forgotten, look into the living word of God, the bible, if it is not written there then it was perverted by man. Spread the good news of Jesus to those that are lost, help them find the correct path, Christian the world needs your help, it is lost

May 4th So many people do not understand the gift that is available through Jesus, and it is free. When you share the gospel don't give up so easily, if not asked to leave the invitation to share what Jesus has done is still open, if in sharing the gospel questions are asked or statements made, that person is crying out, lost from the truth and believing a lie fabricated by satan. That lie is the only truth they know, share the truth of the gospel, remember you are not alone the Trinity stands with you.

May 3rd Where is Jesus when you need Him, assuredly He is right there where ever you have found yourself in need of Him. Jesus will be there whenever you call His name, you can count on Him, the question is can He count on you, He knocks waiting for an answer, waiting for you to invite Him in. He waits in the rain unnoticed, He waits in the cold unnoticed, when we do open the door it is because in many cases we have hit a wall we cannot traverse without Him. Don't wait any longer invite Jesus in, open the door and welcome eternity in, begin living your life as it was meant to be , full of the love of Jesus Christ

May 2nd Looking around at different medias you will never see our God on top, He is there but almost as a hind sight. Aren't you lucky that His love for us keeps us as a fore sight for Him, His day doesn't start with fox or facebook it starts with you, as a matter of fact, according to His word, His day never ends so His thoughts of you never end. God, His Son Jesus, and the Holy Spirit are looking out for you always, never ending, always present. In some cases, waiting for you to acknowledge Them. Their love is great, and They wait on you the created.

May 1st why are you stumbling around in the dark hunting for a light switch, what do you do if you are stumbling around in life? Quit, the answer is find a Savior, and that Savior is Jesus. He will guide your steps throughout the day or night, you will no longer be lost, He is the way, He is the truth, He is the life. Instead of walking around aimlessly accept the Guide that God has provided, you will have purpose for living, and you will be saved. God handed all things over to His Son Jesus with Him you will never again be lost.

Apr 30th What lie have some been told, is there eternity after death, after this body no longer supports life. Many people try to deny that a future exist for them, isn't that sad, nothing to look forward to. The living word of God tells us, and proves it through His Son, what happens after death. People would rather believe a fortune teller than the Creator of this world. Don't pay a charlatan for something that has already been paid for by Jesus Christ, there is a future beside Jesus in eternity, He has conquered the alternative of life in a bottomless pit. Call on Jesus and he will prepare a way for you, He said I go to prepare a way.

Apr 29th When did you start planning for your day today, my wish is for your day to be blessed, why not insure your day is blessed. When you begin plans begin it in prayer to our Father through His Son Jesus Christ. He said all will be given to you, however He will not give you something that you cannot handle, unanswered prayers can be a blessing. Trust in your Lord Jesus Christ as He provides all your needs, not all your wants. Trust Him to guide you and protect you, after all He loves you. Let the Living Word of God provide all your needs, let the Living Word of God protect you from your wants.

Apr 28th Who should come first, the Trinity, to serve one you serve them all. But Jesus served the disciples at the last Passover meal and He said to the disciples do for each other as I have done for you. Examples He has readily revealed in the scriptures. Love each other as I have loved you, love your neighbor as you love yourself. Jesus is all about love, love for His Father in dyeing on the cross because His Father asked it of Him, love for you in paying the price of sin, that squarely belonged to you, and dying at Calvary separated from our Father and His Father because of this sin. One sin is just as great as a trillion sins, Jesus took them all and died with them only to rise again, yes Jesus is Risen.

Apr 27th If you trust in your Lord He will carry you through many times of despair, if you trust in Him He will walk with you down every avenue you go, if you trust in Him He will guide every step you take, if you trust in Him He will never let you slip from His grasp. This is the type of love that exist with Him, however if you decide to walk away He will wait until your return, if you turn and look His arms are stretched out waiting as tears roll down His face, this is also His love for you. Don't go turn and Hug your living Lord and Savior

Apr 26th Deep down in your heart you ask why am I worthy, and deep down in your heart you know you are

God Made You

not. Your heart knows the truth. You knew it before, now and tomorrow. Why did Jesus die for me, He died so that you could live, not just live, live abundantly? As you make your walk with Jesus and this dawns on you, your heart will break because you realize that you are not worthy of the many life's pleasures He brings. As the song says what have I ever done to deserve even one, and the answer is you have done nothing, and you realize you can never do anything, you are redeemed because of the love God has for you, not because of the love you had for Him

Apr 25th, are you going to let man dictate when and how your relationship with our Creator will be, are you going to let man dictate when and how you relate to the only begotten Son of God Jesus? As Jesus said they can do nothing that is not given to them by the Father, o pray to our Lord and Savior when you want because He lives in you, that's right it is a personal relationship, you can talk with Jesus all day and no one will know, all they will know is something is on your mind more important than they are, and one day they may inquire of what it is that often illuminates you, and you can tell them of Jesus Christ. His love will shine through you and Jesus is the only reason for anything.

Apr 24th Looking for the answer, Jesus has the answer, which is exactly how the answer should return to you. The truth is not always what you want to hear, but it is the truth, and it is the answer you need. Jesus is the answer; all things were given into His hands by the Father. Since that is the case, all His answers are true. Don't wish upon a falling star, don't throw a penny in a wishing well, pray to Jesus and believe His will is the only true answer. You see what you want is not always what you need, Jesus holds the answer, and it is true

Apr 23rd Why do we need each other, is it part of a plan? We help each other in understanding and understanding is not a quote it is understanding a quote, it is not a verse, it is understanding a verse. As you begin or continue your walk with Christ you will notice a companion in your walk, you may not see Him but you will feel Him, you may not see Him but you will hear Him. When you accepted Jesus, He gave you a part of Himself in the Holy Spirit which will live in you, as you read the living word of the Father of us all you will be tutored by His spirit and understanding will begin to light your path. Accept the Son and receive acceptance from the Father and receive them in the form of the Holy Spirit, and then all is provided.

Apr 22nd by design everything is different, you are an individual and were designed that way, you were made to be able to choose. When you wake up and look around don't just look at trees, look and notice that they are different, Our Creator did not want robots, He wanted love. You must choose Him, He has already chosen you. Things in this world happen to help you see the light not the darkness, look for the light that illuminates our God and look to Jesus to illuminate the love God has for us. Creation illuminates our Creator and attest to His existence, Jesus illuminates why God created you and it is because He loves you individually and has sent a Savior to bring you Home.

Apr 21st God has promised you many things upon your acceptance of His Son Jesus, so what is the problem.

God Made You

Number one God does not lie, He has said ask and you shall receive, so what is the problem. Number two Jesus said He would never leave you or forsake you, so what is the problem. Number three Jesus provided a guide and prayer partner that lives in you in the Holy Ghost, so what is the problem. Why don't you believe what God has told you, don't let the devil deceive you into thinking you are not worth it, and that is where your doubt is coming from. God said it, it is true.

Apr 20th the three agree, God our creator agrees, Jesus our Savior agrees, and the Holy Spirit agrees, who doesn't agree? They have all chosen you, they all want an intimate relationship with you, why is the created waiting? We are not of this world, this world has nothing to offer in relationship to forever, a marriage is until death do us part, once you accept the Trinity it is a relationship to eternity, They have told you They will never forsake you and this is true. This relationship is nothing but truth, nothing but a love that you have never known, and it is free for the asking and They will live with you forever.

Apr 19th the three agree, God our creator agrees, Jesus our Savior agrees, and the Holy Spirit agrees, who doesn't agree? They have all chosen you, they all want an intimate relationship with you, why is the created waiting? We are not of this world, this world has nothing to offer in relationship to forever, a marriage is until death do us part, once you accept the Trinity it is a relationship to eternity, they have told you They will never forsake you and this is true. This relationship is nothing but truth, nothing but a love that you have never known, and it is free for the asking and They will live with you forever

Apr 18th Why does our God, our Father, our creator gives a lifetime of chances for us to return to Him? Science would have you believe in evolution, they would have you believe the world created you, it did not. Look around you and the world will attest to the one true God. Deception is everywhere and it is all a lie perpetrated by the father of lies using the voices of the lost. Tell the truth, tell of the Gospel of Jesus Christ, the only begotten Son of God, tell of His grace so that they can develop faith through Him and the Holy Spirit.

Apr 17th Everything that was done was done for you, don't continue walking down the blind path that the world has provided for you, you don't have to. There is a redemptive quality that Jesus has provided, and a salvation He has secured. Jesus holds all these things and waits on you. Don't wait until it is too late, if you don't believe now there is a time in the future that you will believe. Accept what your Lord has obtained for you, don't be deceived by satan he only has one mission which is for you to believe his lie

Apr 16th Jesus has risen, Jesus has risen after He accomplished what the Father asked of Him. Because of Jesus's choice to honor His Father and Our Father you are saved. It started in the garden, at the false arrest at night, it was finished at the cross, but He didn't stop there. He conquered the grave He conquered death. His accomplishments are yours, accept His free gift of salvation, He paid the price, you can reap the reward. Truly repent in your heart and accept Jesus as your Savior and you will be set free.

God Made You

Apr 15th God our Creator said rest. He knows the needs of your body and Spirit, so rest. When He provides time rest, rest in the assurance that you will occupy a mansion one day, rest in the truth that Jesus is your Savior, rest in the bond between you and Jesus which is the Holy Spirit. Jesus said that the Sabbath is for man, so rest. Rest rejuvenates your spirit which rejuvenates your body and prepares you to minister to others, don't let your friends walk blindly down a road that leads to damnation. So, rest and share the Gospel of Jesus. The Father, Son, and Holy Spirit wants everyone to have the opportunity for Salvation, so rest and rejuvenate so you can share Jesus with everyone

Apr 14th, Do you hear His voice this morning, listen to see if you recognize it? He said My sheep know my voice. We were created by our Shepard and we all know His voice, all the noise of this world tries to drown out His voice, listen and don't be distracted and you will hear Him. The problem is we have been apart so long that we are being deceived into thinking this world is our shepard and not the one true living God. Deception comes in many forms but if you just listen you will hear and remember, Jesus came to earth to remind us of where we truly came from, and has left the Holy Spirit to assist us in our return, through grace from the Father, delivered by the Son we are saved. Listen and you will hear

Apr 13th Jesus is coming in your lifetime, when you leave this body the next body you will be in will be new and you will be with Jesus. When you go to sleep, you will be with Him when you awake you meet Him because He said He will return for you, and that is truth. For all of us that believe in Jesus and accepted Him as our Lord and Savior the end of this life in this world begins a new life with Him, for us there is only one death. Tell someone today about Jesus so they will not take part in the second death, a death that has no ending

Apr 12th don't let the world blind you into thinking this is all you have to look forward to, don't let time slip through the palms of your hands. Jesus said one day it will be too late, He said He comes as a thief in the night. Once he returns for those of us that are in the grave it is too late to make the decision of acceptance. You say I have a lifetime, and you do from the day your born to the day you die. Not one in the world can tell you when you die, but Jesus can assure you that you will never die. Accept him and be assured that you are one of His He told He was going to prepare a home for, don't trust the world trust the Lord

Apr 11^{th,} Do we deserve the grace that God gave us, would we choose Him if Jesus had not died on the cross? We were blind to our Fathers glory until Jesus shed the curtain between us and eternity, Jesus did this so our relationship with God could begin anew. As God watches and waits for us to decide to return to Him, He sacrificed His only begotten Son so you could make a decision to return to Him, without Jesus you have no right or rights. God so loved the world, if you have not made the decision to accept Jesus, make it. If you know someone who needs to make that decision help them find Jesus, they are truly lost without Him

Apr 10^{th,} Have you made your plans for today, start by talking with your Savior and Lord Jesus Christ? Starting with Jesus helps to illuminate some of the non-essentials, things which steer you down a path which ends in after thoughts of why did I do that. After all His Spirit which lives in you will bring things which are detrimental to your soul into the light, while these activities seem fun at the time the route they are on take you into the ways of the world and you will begin to lose perspectives of truth and begin to believe a lie. Jesus is the truth and the life, without His grace you are on a road called Despair.

Apr 9th Just relax today knowing that all things are in the hands of a loving God. He has sent His angels to look out for you, God has sent the Holy Spirit to watch out for you, our Father sent His only Son to pay a price of redemption you could not pay. You are the most important person on His mind, yet some choose to reject the truth today, share the truth of Heaven today, share the truth of a loving God today, share the gospel of Jesus today. Everything you see attest to Fathers existence, let your tongue attest to the truth of our Savior, redeemer, and King Jesus Christ today

Apr 8th not yet we can still tell the seasons, Jesus said there will be signs of His return. Don't wait till it is too late to accept Him for who He is, why do people wait to have a love as deep and fulfilling as the Love Jesus has for you. Because of you Jesus conquered the cross, Jesus conquered the grave, Jesus conquered the temptations that we cannot. His strength can be your strength, He said His yoke is light, why carry the weight of the world when He already is. He said His yoke is light, oh what a friend we have in Jesus

Apr 7th Jesus showed us how to love, how to care, how to live for one another, the examples He has shown us are true. Don't say yes, I know but I don't deserve it, don't try to explain a gift of love from our Creator, and you are right you don't deserve the grace He gives us, but the explanation is not for you to figure out. His love for you is all you need to know, you need only accept Jesus gift and know that he is your Redeemer, your Savior, and your Lord, knowing you cannot return to the Father but by way of the Son, He is the way, He is the truth, and He is your only ticket home, and it is all free.

Apr 6th as you walk in faith and you fail Jesus is there to help you back on your feet, don't give up. The world is always calling for you to return to its turmoil, but remember you are never alone. Sometimes it feels as if you are walking alone but the Good Shepard is coming back for you, Jesus watches over you always and intervenes to save you, His love for you never wanes, it is true to you always. Call on and trust the name above all names Jesus

Apr 5th If you feel as if something or someone is calling for you, don't ignore it, someone is and it is the Spirit of the one true God. You may at first try to ignore this feeling, thank God that He is persistent. You see His love for you is so great that He will never forget about you. The knock is continuous and you hear it, don't ignore it, open the door, don't ignore eternity, it is forever. God has provided away through His Own Son to redeem you, They love you and want you to accept them, you have a destination after your body dies, make sure it is the one you want.

Apr 4th it is sometime so hard to understand why, but if you believe that our hope is in Jesus, He was prepared, He said that He went to prepare and really, He went to prepare for our homecoming, He said He would not leave us nor forsake us and that means from the day you accepted him as your Savior to eternity. He walks with us always and He knows were to step and you will not have fear or pain because were ever we go He has been there before, is Father, our God said you will always have away, trust in the Trinity of God, Jesus, and the Holy Spirit, all three are present and with you.

Apr 3rd God knew from the beginning of creation the sacrifice of His Son would have to happen for the great sin of disobedience which we committed in the Garden. God was willing to suffer for us, and Jesus was willing to suffer for us. Jesus did the time in hell for us, while He was there He conquered death, and He returned to His former glory beside His Father in Heaven. Jesus did not do this for the love we had for Him, He did it for the love He had for the Father, He did it for the love He had for us. Jesus paid the debt of sin in full. Don't let satan deceive you, there is nothing you need to add to this debt, all you need to do is accept the gift given freely from Jesus Christ, it is finished and it can be yours.

Apr 2nd, isn't it amazing that all the answers are in the Bible, many times after rereading the word of God you say I never saw that before, why is that. The bible says God draws you to His Son Jesus, and the words of bible lead us to Him. As you begin your journey that ends in redemption you are given a guide through the Holy Spirit, He helps you as you read the words of our creator and illuminates the answers you are searching for. You were never alone, but you have to make a choice, serve a King who is at the right hand side of the thrown of God or serve the world, the price has been paid and a guide to eternity provided, you must accept Jesus for who He is, the only begotten Son of God

God Made You

Apr 1st Trust Jesus with all your needs don't look at the world and thank your going to find peace because there is no peace to be found without Jesus. God sacrificed his only begotten son so that you can be redeemed, repent and call on the name of Jesus and you will be saved

Mar 31st Another day to find the path to righteousness, a path that is straight and narrow, we are not capable of walking this path alone, we need help. This path leads to beauty and peace, things we can only dream about. There is a way, and there is a guide. This guide is named Jesus, and His way is true, He watches every step you take on this path and gently assist you as you begin to fall. Sometimes you leave this path and walk away as you get lost, but He has a light you can see no matter how dim it becomes, call out to Jesus and you will see immediately the steps you need to take to return to the path, because it is His path and He knows you cannot do it alone. Walk with Him and live.

Mar 30th Today, find rest through Jesus, His name gives peace and joy. Without His presence in your life you are lost to the ever-changing tides of this world and turmoil awaits around every turn. His path is straight because there is nothing to hide, He is all truth and his ways are proven and enable you to walk assuredly. Hold your head high because you are walking with the only King this world has ever known and He has chosen you. What the world has to offer is for naught, but what Jesus has to offer is for eternity

God Made You

Mar 29th Let's get up and prepare ourselves for the day, makeup, clothes, diet, exercise, everything you can see in the mirror. All that preparation for the outside doesn't do anything for the real need of the body. Our fathers word clearly says that all the preparation you see in the mirror is last, first is to prepare your spirit. How do you accomplish this, first seek your Lord and Savior Jesus Christ? Eternity is forever and Jesus is the only path back to a union with our creator. Your body will not inherit eternity, but your spirit will. You will be given a new body that needs no preparation, there will be no flaws. You will be perfect in Jesus, and He prepares a way for us to reunite with God and eternity.

Mar 28th, it is time to begin another day, what task are pressing, what burdens lie ahead, can you find peace, can you find rest in another hectic day? Jesus said come to Him and you will find peace, Jesus said come to Him and find rest, It is true, but you must trust in Him. Oh, there are so many added benefits like salvation, someone who will never leave you or forsake you, a King who will guide you to eternity as He provides you a mansion forever. Jesus will give you rest, accept Him, He is your personal Savoir, He is the only begotten Son of God, and He loves you with an unquenchable love.

Mar 27th, You may change your mind, Gods mind is already made up, for He so loved the world that He gave up His only begotten Son. The world does not love you, God loves you. So many people are lost and see no proof of His existence, the mountains speak of His existence, the oceans speak of His existence, anything you see speaks of our Fathers existence, to deny this truth is to deny that you exist. All truths may not be able to be proven by man, but they are still truths. His Son Jesus spoke of His existence, yet so many people are lost to the deception of satan. Tell the world of the gospel of Jesus Christ, share the truth.

Mar 26th Why me what have I ever done to deserve even one of the many life's blessings God gives, comes from a song but the answer is you have done nothing, you can do nothing, you are not capable. Jesus Christ has done everything that will ever have to be done to justify you to His Father. Jesus said on the cross before He died it is finished, some of the synonyms for finished is over, done, complete, you cannot add or subtract anything, accept this gift of love. Don't continue through your life without Jesus, He is the only way

Mar 25th, you say prove your love, first He created you, second, He died for you, third He conquered death for you. Jesus stated if this cup could pass, but not my will, your will be done, that was after the humiliation he was handed by the religious leaders of the day during His witnessing of His Father and your Creator. Jesus chose to do what His Father had asked and His Father asked because of the love He had for you, Jesus chose to do what He did because of the love He had for you. After Jesus was resurrected and returned to the very throne of God His Father imagine the party, and when you return to the Father through His Son Jesus the party will be just as extravagant, all of this because of true love, a love that is ever quenching.

Mar 24th No matter how you feel about yourself there is someone who loves you unconditionally, His name is Jesus. As you think about yourself and how great or miserable your life is going He is watching you and just waiting for you to notice, Jesus has His hand reaching out for you, to congratulate you or console you. His love for you is so great He would wait a lifetime for you, and during your lifetime He will never pull His hand of comfort away from you. It is all up to you, His hand and love is forever, His love for you is perfect. His knock is persistent, you may not hear it, you may not respond because life is noisy, but He is still knocking, He waits on you to listen, look, and open the door of your heart.

Mar 23rd Why do people choose to try to live this life on their own, we are made to love and help each other, God did not create us to be alone. In your search don't accept the answers of any man who does not know Gods ways, he will mislead you because he knows no better than the ways of a world that is misled by the devil, there is one man which you can turn to and find the fellowship you are looking for and His name is Jesus. He has already proven His love for you, and all His words are true, He said He will never leave you or forsake you, and He never will. He lives in you forever, He cares for everything about you, you can find no deeper love, If you are searching ask Him in and your life will change to wonderful instead of wandering.

Mar 22nd, Do you feel secure, how did you sleep last night? Thank God today, He was watching over you. If the entire world, including the spiritual, was not limited by God you would not have slept very well if at all. Satan cannot do anything without God allowing it, but if he was not restricted, you child of God would stay in his crosshairs. Remember you cannot serve two masters, serve the only Master that insures your security, serve the only God who chose to send His Son Jesus to redeem you from this world and paid the price to free you from your captivity, oh the love They have for you.

Mar 21st Be amazed, look how wonderful our God is, look how wonderful His love for you is. Even while you are under indictment for your sins, even while He is starting to give a judgment you can cry out to Him, and through His Son Jesus Christ He will forgive you. Don't wait to the last minute, begin a wonderful life with Jesus today and watch as blessings flow from the throne of Heaven as the relationship that was lost in the garden of Eden was found and began to be paid for in another garden as Jesus was arrested. This love that God, Jesus and the Holy Spirit has for us is overflowing, accept the gift of life through Jesus.

Mar 20th If you are having a problem with life search the word of God, regarding life every question you have has an answer. Read the bible and you will find that it contains all truths. Accept Jesus and you will receive a tutor in the form of the Holy Spirit, and will be given insight which will guide you to Heaven. It starts with a relationship with Jesus and ends with an eternity living in all happiness, all love, and all contentment. You will find that reality is complete through Jesus, He is the corner stone to a foundation of love.

Mar 19th, did you know that God our Father, our personal and individual Creator, knew from the beginning of creation that He would have to send His only begotten Son through the agony of crucifixion, that He would have to send His Son named Jesus through the valley of the shadow of death alone? So much for the Father of a Savior and King to ask, but Jesus said not my will but your will be done. God did not need a Savior, Jesus did not need a Savoir, you needed a Savior and because of a love that is eternal God provided a Savoir, man is not suited to be a Savior and will never be, man is only suitable to be saved and man's Savior is Jesus, tell Him of your love for Him this morning. Your Rescuer, Redeemer, Protector, and Deliverer

Mar 18th Wake up with a prayer this morning, a prayer of thanks for what Jesus did for you. Ask what the things you should focus on today. Jesu already knows where you are heading, and how you are going to get there. Put Jesus on your side as you go through life, there will be bumps but He will prepare you for these events. He knows them and will not allow for you to be stopped, He will not allow you to be tempted beyond what you can handle and He always provides a way to escape. With Jesus, the adversary who is the Devil will not succeed, he did not succeed at the cross, and with Jesus he will not succeed against you, Carry the love for Jesus and that love will be returned to you 100 fold. The love Jesus has for you has no comparison.

Mar 17th The absence of Jesus is the absence of everything, so many of man's religions try to discount who are Savior is, why, because He is the God given solution to man's problem with eternity. Man was created to live forever, the body may die, but you will never die. The adversary, the accuser, Satan, the devil, knows the Creator, he knows how we were designed, and what we were designed for, he knows our purpose. Our purpose is to praise Jesus, to praise his Father, to live with our Creator forever, to feel the love God has for us. So, Satan lies, he is the father of lies, and deceives us, he blinds us from the truth with something that resembles the truth. Jesus is the truth, Jesus is the way, Jesus is the life. There is only one way Jesus.

Mar 16th God does have a way of showing man who He is, open your eyes and see how man tries to predict the future. We often look at the weather on the news and find that the forecast is off by a mile. God's word hold true today, yesterday and tomorrow. If you want to know the future read His word, how do I know for the Bible tells me so. Don't go to a fortune teller who knows nothing, don't look at your zodiac sign for wisdom, the Bible cannot be proven false, why, because it is all true. The Author of the Bible is available for clarification also, and will send the Holy Spirit to assist you in all aspects of His word. Look to the Author of life rather at life for answers. Accept Jesus and everything begins to clear.

Mar 15th Lonely, you're not alone, Jesus sent His Spirit to assist you, Listen to Him and He will not stir you wrong, He will help you in your walk with Jesus, He will comfort you when you fell there is no escape. You will never be alone as old friends from the world stop to tempt you to walk in darkness, the Holy Spirit will help you deny temptations and transgression against God. The Holy Spirit will help you serve our Risen Savoir and eventually as your walk with Jesus continues you will want to speak of Jesus first instead of trivial pursuits. He will become a friend above all friends. Your life with the Trinity will become personal because of a love instead of a need.

Mar 14th What do you have to look forward to today, it is not the cross, it is not judgement for every sin that the world has or will commit, it is not separation from the Father, it is not three days of walking through the valley of the shadow of death and conquering it on your own. Accept the one that paid that price for you, accept Jesus Christ as your Savior and Lord, know Him for who He is, the only begotten Son of God who left Heaven to live the life of a man without sin to pay a price He did not owe because of love for His Father, and because of love for you. Jesus is your Redeemer.

Mar 13th Any time, any situation, whenever He is needed, Jesus is there. Jesus instituted the original open door policy, He is available to you always. You are His only concern, He died on a cross and conquered death to show you that you are first. Accept Jesus and He said He will never leave you nor forsake you, can you say this to Him? You have assurance that His words are true by two witnesses, His Father and His Spirit that lives in you. Look what He did to prove His love, there is no greater love.

Mar 12th Time is important to you and I, we worry about this thing called a bucket list. Don't let your bucket list become your downfall in life. The bucket list doesn't include Jesus, my bet is there is not one that includes him. We need to quit worrying about life and what we did not accomplish, there are more important things and they include death. Include Jesus in your bucket list and your bucket list will change from this world to eternity. You will rewrite your bucket list and find grace, you will get fulfillment instead of accomplishment. Your eyes will be opened to the important things on your bucket list, so put finding Jesus first on your list and He will also be the last thing on your list, your life will be fulfilled

Mar 11th Wake up this morning ready to serve your master, but remember you can only serve one master. Start with prayer with Jesus and the Father of Jesus. When you pray, pray in humility, but be specific to whom you are praying. The devil is also the father, the father of lies, so be specific when you are praying. The Holy Spirit will help you, the spirit of Jesus will help you pray to Jesus who has opened the throne of God to all that have accepted Him. Serve your neighbors with the love of the Gospel, follow the example of Jesus Christ .

Mar 10th Everyone has a solution, everyone has the answer, everyone seems to know what to do. Everything suggested is different so how can anyone of them be right. There is only one subject matter expert in all of heaven and earth and He has a name, it is Jesus. He has already been through what you have been through and survived, even to death and back. He has left written instructions with all the answers. Read and study the owner's manual which was written for you from your creator, every answer to every question is there, it wasn't written to deceive you it was written to fulfill you, it was written with love

Mar 9th Why were you created as an individual, why do you think on your own? Our creator created you for one reason, to share His undying love with you. He gave you chooses after the fall from the garden. He gave you away to justify yourself, through Jesus who paid the price for you, or you will pay the price yourself which you cannot because you don't have the capacity to pay the price. So, accept the price that was already paid by Jesus by accepting Him, or pay it yourself. Just remember self will take an eternity to pay for the sins that rightly belong to self.

Mar 8th Today thank Jesus for what he did for you, bludgeoned, beaten, scourged, humiliated, and hung on a tree, because of you and for you. Thank God today for what He did for you, He watched His only begotten son Jesus go through all of this and because of His love for you did not intervene, as a matter of fact He requested this of His Son for you. The Trinity loves you and waits for your return and when you do return there is rejoicing in heaven

God Made You

Mar 7th God hears your prayers, he has always heard your prayers, he longs for the reunion we had that was lost in the Garden. He hears your hearts request and will draw you to His only begotten Son, He hears our prayers for unity with Him and longs for it. He has provided a way when there was no way, you must choose Jesus and in so doing you accept the God Head and an eternity with Them

Mar 6th get interested in eternity because it is real. You are going to live forever, that is a fact you have no choice about, your choice is where you will spend it. Here are your two choices, in heavenly bliss or the pity of the bottomless pit, the lake of fire, an eternity in a life of misery. Choice heaven by choosing Jesus who holds the key, He purchased your ticket, and He will personally escort you to a mansion He built and has your name on it, accept Him as your Lord and Savior and rest in His loving caress.

Mar 5th When you wake up in the morning it is hard to get started, it is even harder when it is not a work day. We think a cup of coffee will help revive us, but it is a stimulant that doesn't last. When you wake up begin with a conversation with our Savoir Jesus Christ, in starting with Him you are engaging the Father and the Holy Spirit all at once. You are receiving a stimulant for life and that's love through the Trinity. Because of this love you will find that you want to share it, share it with the world and begin a revival of passion for one another.

Mar 4th, do you think you can find wisdom here on earth, sure man honors men and women, but is that wisdom, is it total wisdom? Without the originator of wisdom, it is not wisdom. The full plan for wisdom is already outlined in

God's living word and the reward is out of this world and your treasures will never tarnish or collect dust. Perfect wisdom, perfect knowledge all come from the Trinity, all from the creators of everything seen and unseen, the Father, Son, and the Holy Spirit. Accept Jesus and accept all Three.

Mar 3rd To decide, to make a commitment, to walk with Jesus, Things will still happen, but know this, you will never be alone. Man, will leave you, man will forsake you, Jesus said He will never leave you or forsake you, His vows are true, He will never turn from you, there is not a possibility of divorce. Moses gave that for man because the commitment did not last, Jesus's is forever, make your commitment forever, accept Him as Lord.

Mar 2nd There are consequences to the mistakes we make, because we fell from perfection in the garden, our mistakes affect others. The Father Abba makes no mistakes, everything He creates is perfect including giving us the right to choose, he did not nor want to create robots. He created you for fellowship with Him and each other. His Son Jesus redeemed you through crucifixion so that you could return to Gods original plan, His plan never changed, He knew the sacrifices He and Jesus would have to make for you from the beginning and through this amazing love He has for you He gave you the opportunity for eternal life with Him. God makes no mistakes, He wants you to choose Him

Mar 1st be assured that your relationship with God is complete, so many things will seem to take precedence, the reality is they are all attempts to turn your face from His. Jesus paid the price for that renewed relation and He offers it to you freely. This is what it assures you of, in eternity you will be with Him and there is no nashing of teeth, there is no crying, there is no bad news. This world is not the end, it is the beginning. Jesus is the answer to everything, set your eyes on Him, put Him first. His love will abound in you, and through you

Feb 28th, you must make a choice, to accept your Lord and Savior Jesus the Son of the only living God that ever existed or not. It is not as simple as not making that choice either, by not choosing, you are choosing. Recognize Jesus for who He is, life will be so much easier and you will find purpose. He has accepted you for who you are, go to Him as you are today and He will prepare you for an eternal life with Him

Feb 27th there are many words in the dictionary and man gave them a definition. God also has a dictionary with definitions, such as loyalty which is defined with one word Jesus, He was loyal to His Father and went to the cross. Love is also defined with one word, Jesus, He so loved the world He gave His only begotten Son. Truth, Jesus, He is true to all that believe in Him. We could go on for days and Jesus will still be the answer, believe in Him and live an eternity

Feb 26th God filled you with your spirit, with your life, and you are an individual. He did not create you from a mold. You are the only you in existence and He loves you. He created you for fellowship with Him. As a matter of fact, He longed for the return of that relationship, after man was deceived in the garden, that He gave His only begotten Son to revive it. He also gave you free will to accept or not accept Him for who He is, and Jesus for who He is. Jesus paid a price for you, a price that returns the relationship you should have with God, accept all that has been paid, accept Jesus as your Lord and Savior

Feb 25th man, will tell you to find a job that you enjoy and it won't seem like a job at all, guess what, it isn't a job to Jesus to watch over you, it's a want. He wants to comfort you, He wants to teach you, He wants to be a part of your life. If you have chosen Him He has even given you a part of Himself, His own Spirit. His Spirit justifies you, Jesus justifies you, and the Father wants you. All three love you with the same intensity, accept all of Them and be set free

Feb 24th what are you looking for, the creator has provided a way, and has made that way available to everyone. We cannot except this reward of salvation and grace because we have done nothing to deserve it. There is no catch to what Jesus did on the cross for us, He died for our transgressions so we could go directly to His Father and our Father, He conquered death so we are no longer captives, we are free, and He came out of the grave and returned to the Fathers side to assure we had an appointment with eternity in Heaven. There is nothing to do, except Jesus for who He is and what He did

Feb 23rd receive the gift that will never grow old, that will never tarnish or discolor, the gift that looks and feels brand new every day. Man, cannot make it although he attempts to deceive you into thinking he can. There is only one way to receive this gift which is also free, there is no cost, it was already purchased for you. Accept Jesus Christ as your Savior and King and everything you seek will have a brilliance that is beyond beautiful because His gift of life is completeness

Feb 22nd the adversary will use every opportunity to take your focus of the One True Living God. He will make the most joyful event into naught to pull you away from Jesus. Keep your eyes on Jesus and look to Him for all wisdom and Knowledge, He will not steer you wrong, He can only steer you toward an eternal life with Him. Remember there are two eternity's, one is of the Father, the other is with Satan. Jesus's path is straight and true, follow Him and allow Him to take you to an eternity of love and light in the presence of our Heavenly Father.

Feb 21st as you look at the world today, take in all the headlines, it is a sure thing you will find chaos. Look toward the Holy of Holies and you will find serenity. At the Fathers throne, there is nothing but love. Strife is an activity of this world He created and we destroyed. There is peace with the Son Jesus, He is the only way to the throne. Men that don't know Jesus creates chaos, without His Spirit we are lost, all men are looking for eternity but most do not know how to get to an eternity of peace and love, that way is given through Jesus

Feb 20th If you are looking for stability, look toward the creator. After the fall man has no stability, as a matter of fact, after the fall man lost many things. Yes, we were created in Gods image but this world and sin has flawed all of us. We need to return to the Father to regain His image, and the way back is through His only begotten Son Jesus. Bring back the nature of God, the purpose of the creator. Accept Jesus as your Savior and Lord and then commune with the Trinity

God Made You

Feb 19th Here you are at the beginning of the week, what do you have to look forward to, just work? Jesus said love your neighbor as yourself. Go see your neighbors as you have time, share the good news of Jesus with them. Jesus also says serve them, so ask if there is any way that you can help them. Take time to serve Jesus, we don't have time because we choose not to make time. If we are willing, He is more than able. Love each other, just like Jesus loves us. As you share your love, just as Jesus shared His love, soon you will find that your neighbors will begin to share their love. Be an inspiration to each other, just as Jesus is an inspiration to us

Feb 18th overwhelming, it doesn't seem to stop, you can't keep up with it all, turn to Jesus. Don't just glance His way, turn and look fully into the face of Jesus, and stop. Believe in who He is and He will take your burdens from you, He said He would never forsake you, and He won't' He will fully lift you and carry you through the shadow of death. His love will not leave you, you are a precious jewel of love. Give yourself fully over to Him so He can love you. He is the Savior and King.

Feb 17th Nothing in this world is a sure thing , there are no promises that can be kept. Man may have good intentions but cannot assure you they will follow through. Nothing on earth is for sure. If you want a to be sure that a promise will be kept look to the creator not the created. Jesus said He would never forsake you and His words are completion. He said it is finished on the cross,He doesn't just mean your salvation, He means everything. His love is complete

Feb 16th do you think that you can do it on your own, you can't. This void everyone has need to be filled and you will fill it. The what is the question, the world will fill this void in your heart, but it is superficial and quickly needs to be replenished. Fill your Heart with Living Water and you will never thirst again. Jesus never needs to be replenished, that void will stay full to overflowing, you can never empty the love He has for you, If you fall, drink from His well of Living Water and you will be replenished without failure. His love is so deep for you and His water is so refreshing

Feb 15th agape love is a Greek word that describes an eternity of definitions for love, only the Trinity can display such a love. The three are willing to give you this love, all you must do is ask. There is no reason to go through life miserable, when the cure of Jesus is waiting to give you a full pardon. So, put off the Adamic nature of the world and put on the Spiritual nature of Jesus

Feb 14th When you accept Jesus as your Savior, and become a child of God, you will never be involved in controversy again. All your life will begin to evolve around His glory and grace. You will realize the love that is surrounding you is not superficial but as deep as eternity. The adversary would want you to believe a lie, you will quickly conclude that there is only truth in this relationship you have found in Jesus. The King now has you, and His love will never let you go.

God Made You

Feb 13th When you are a child of God you can expect miracles every day. They come from small to large, but they come. Open your hearts, mind, and sciences and you will start noticing them on a regular basis. Jesus said ask and you shall receive. Open your eyes because His miracles are not limited to this world, He loves you and is with you always

Feb 12th what benefit is it to you to walk alone through this maze called life, without direction you will have no direction. Many people will enter your life attempting to steer you this way or that way. There is only one way to walk and that way is to walk with our Lord Jesus Christ. He will not leave you or forsake, and His words are true. In fact when you walk with Him He will provide a piece of Himself, His own Spirit to comfort you and be with you always. If you fall He will pick you up. Love and follow Jesus

Feb 11th Look in the mirror, don't deny what you see, it is an image of the Creator. Some would have you believe that this is not true. That falsehood began with the father of lies, he wants you to think that you are not special. Talk with Jesus and He will tell you the truth. He loves you and created you for a purpose, and that purpose is with Him and our Heavenly Father God

Feb 10th where do you look to make you happy, what do you read to carry you through the day, how can you help yourself. Look to our only Savior for happiness and you will become happy, read the written word of our Father, accept Jesus then look for His Spirit within you to help you, comfort you, teach you, and yes carry you. This love the Trinity has for you is beyond this world and it is yours if you ask you will receive

Feb 9th to our Lord Jesus all of us are beautiful inside and out, He made us this way. You are perfect. He knows all the flaws that man established after creation and he can fix all of them with a tune up of the heart. So many people, both possessed or not, keep saying we can fix you, they cannot. The only fix which will last an eternity is our Savior, our Redeemer, our King, Jesus

Feb 8th why does man try to explain the unexplainable. We have all kinds of explanations as to why. Point to the only reason for everything, that reason is Jesus. Our Father created everything to glorify His only begotten Son. Nothing created can fulfil His role as Redeemer and Savior. Man, would want you to believe everything, when your heart really is only willing to believe one truth Jesus is Lord

Feb 7th, you can do many things that keep you from seeing Jesus, and you can act as if reality is not real. Reality is different from what you think it is, Jesus can see every mistake that you have ever made and He still loves you, He heard every word that you ever said and He still loves you, He was there in every place you have ever went and He still loves you. Jesus is still knocking because despite everything He still loves you

Feb 6th things happen every day and people watch, what is important? The world will keep us so occupied with nothing that we do not see what is important. Jesus waits for the one revelation that will open your eyes to the love He has for you. Then we realize that all the glitz and glam of this world is nothing. We realize that the King does have the whole world in His hands. Share this truth, share the Gospel

Feb 5th, did you make plans for today, and did you pray about them. Include God in all your plans, don't forget Him, He certainly has not forgotten you. His plans from the beginning of creation included you. When He sent Jesus to the cross His plan included you. When Jesus sent His Holy Spirit, His plan included you. When Jesus our King returns, His plan will include you. The wonderful and loving thing about His plans are that they are all about you, include the Father and His Son in your plans and you cannot go wrong

Feb 4th God is watching over you. He is concerned about every step you take. He is with you where ever you go. There is no where you can go that He has not been. You can trust Him with your life.

Feb 3rd Jesus, who is our Savior and King, doesn't start or finish with one emotion or another, He starts with love and finishes with love. All His love is dedicated to you. Believe in Him, He will not fail you ever, He does not change His mind. He is always knocking even if you at first reject Him, He continues knocking. Open the door

Feb 2nd there are two ways to eternity, one is a lie told by the father of lies, the other is the truth told by our Abba, Father, our God. One is a large road with many routes that end up at one point, a lake of fire. The other is a straight narrow road that ends up with God and an eternal life with Him. That way has an admission and that is Jesus, without Him there is no admittance, but once you begin to follow

Him he will never let you go, He will be with you forever, He will walk with you all the way throughout eternity

Feb 1st everyday pray to God through His Son Jesus as you continue your life with Him. Read His written word and find wonderful guidance that came through our Father Abba God Himself. There are so many ways to know the truth, He did not leave us ignorant. He has provided Himself, He has provided Jesus, and He has provided the Holy Spirit which lives in all the children of God. Listen to His word and become enlightened by His wisdom, He is our Creator

Jan 31st do not think for a moment that what you say and do does not matter to our Savior Jesus, our King Jesus, the only begotten Son of God Jesus. Every breath you take is counted by Him. You may not know Him but every movement you make is counted by Him. Without His sacrifice, you would not exist today, there would not be a choice to be made, choice the gift of eternal life He provided for you on that hill where He was crucified

Jan 30th everyone wants something given to them for free, and the greatest gift that you could ever receive is free. Jesus went to the cross to give you that gift, you only need to accept it in your heart and eternity is assured to you. Not for what you did but what your Savior did for you. He did this because this was the Fathers will, and so it was His will also. The Son only does what the Father has shown Him. His love is free

Jan 29th why doesn't everyone know Jesus, He has extended His comforting hand to all. And for those that heard His knock and opened their hearts to Him have found purpose, and love, and grace. Don't march behind man's banners, march behind Jesus' banner of love, grace, truth, abundant life, someone who always makes your cause number one. Be for Him and He will tell the Father of your love, follow Jesus

Jan 28th man was created to praise the creator, the problem is to many are now seeking to receive the praise for something that only belongs to our Lord. Nothing we see, do, or hear is possible without our Lord's support, the problem is when the created perverts what was created. God said on the day of rest it is good, creation was perfect, made by a perfect creator, yet man still chooses to pervert perfection. We need not make a decision that has already been made and perfected by an all knowing, all loving God, come back to the Father through His Son Jesus, He is the only perfection we need or will ever need

Jan 27th what do we spend our time on, everything seems like it is a priority. there is not enough time in the day. Change your perspective, a thousand years is like a day, and a day is like a thousand years. Use Gods time line and life will fall in to place, use Jesus as the Beginning and the End and you will find that those little life emergencies will start to fade away as you realize that Who is important and what is not

Jan 26th, are you prepared for today, God preordained today for you. He knows every aspect of today, your day. Wouldn't you rather trust in Jesus who has already sent His

Spirit to assist you with events which are 100% known by Him, or do you want to trust the world to deal with whatever hand unfolds. Don't let Satan throw kinks in an already well laid out plan, rebuke him and he will leave you. Jesus is the answer to all your needs

Jan 25th, you were created to praise God, everything we see was created by God to praise Him, not only praise Him, but praise Him through His only Son Jesus. Jesus died on the cross to praise His Father. Jesus came to fulfill a request from our Creator, not forced but asked, which was to conquer what we brought into our life in the Garden of Eden, which is death. We have a chance to return to our original estate which is fellowship with our Lord through the actions of His Son. Accept Jesus

Jan 24th what purpose does someone have that doesn't know Jesus as their Savior, they have no direction, A circle has no beginning or end, and you always end up back at the same spot, The straight and narrow path which Jesus speaks of has a beginning, which is you, and it has an ending, which is an eternal life with our King and Redeemer Jesus Christ

Jan 23rd everyone is looking for stability, and so many cannot find it. They only need to look to the King, cocreator with our Father who art in Heaven. Most do not know of His Glory, of His Grace, or that He capable of saving all. He is the only one that truly came, saw, and conquered, He is King. Accept Him and your life will change

Jan 22nd Everyone you see God loves, why because Jesus paid for our sins and God pardoned our transgressions.

God Made You

Because of the actions of His Son, we are forgiven. God knows the potential of all His creation and He allows us the freedom to choose. The word choice is where the problem lies, you can murder yourself by not accepting Jesus, or you can live for eternity through Him. There is no Jury to decide for you, that decision is yours. The evidence is present all around you of His Glory, accept and praise Him forever

Jan 21st wake up and look around at everything that is familiar to you and praise the Lord. You are protected by Him and He is always present. Pray to Him and remain mindful that Jesus is always with you. God, Jesus, and the Holy Ghost are all the same in thought and purpose and that purpose is to extend all the love they hold to you. More than a Mother has for her child. This is a love that knows no bounds including death, that price was paid for you

Jan 20th God made you, and He made you perfect. The world brought imperfection to you. He sent Jesus to bring perfection out of imperfection, and He has. Acceptance of Jesus is the cure to imperfection, their very robe is light, They have nothing to hide, there are no flaws. When you accept Jesus as your Savoir and King, you commit to Him, He was already committed to you. Even the fine lines of imperfection will begin to fade away

Jan 19th look at yourself and remember who you were created by, stop and listen for Gods voice. You will find that His memory is not from the far past, but it is the voice of the present. Jesus said He would never leave you or forsake you. Never is eternal and He created eternity. He created so His relationship with you would be forever. Oh, the friend we have in Jesus, His love is everlasting

Jan 18th one day we will all figure it out, nothing the Father our God created can be added to or built upon, He said everything is very good. Jesus said it is complete, as He sacrificed Himself in our place. There is nothing left to improve upon, but man keeps on trying and claiming they can do it better. Praise the Creator not the created. Man, had no part in creation only the Father, His Son, and their Holy Spirit. Praise them and pray only to them

Jan 17th what does it mean that our Lord Jesus Christ bought us with a price, it would have been so easy to have paid with monies, but no we assured that it would not be that easy. We sold our selves to the accuser. Bless our King He was still willing to pay a price of blood. When you were created, you were not created cheaply, you were created with the very breath of God. Our savoir paid with the highest price ever conceived, His very life. He has walked through the valley of death and conquered it, pray He walks with you, and He will

Jan 16th there is only one King to honor, and that is Jesus the only begotten Son of the Father. When is His day of remembrance, He does not have one, why? because we serve a living King, an eternal King, a King that will never forsake us or leave us. Our King is not dead, He is alive and we need to think of Him and thank Him every second of every day

Jan 15th, it is not hard to follow our Savoir and Lord Jesus Christ, He has provided all that is needed, he created a Spirit to comfort you. He created legions upon legions of

God Made You

angels to protect you. He created this beautiful love he blesses you with, you cannot go wrong when you follow Jesus because He knows you, the Father and the Holy spirit, and Jesus created you. You only need to love Them back

Jan 14th guess who has been watching over you, the very Spirit of our risen Lord and Savior Jesus. He said He would never leave you or forsake you, to insure this He was crucified for our transgressions and resurrected after He defeated all that stands in our way as we continue to His Father and eternity. He has given to those that trust Him His very own Spirit to insure us of His devotion to us.

Jan 13th make time for the most important decision of your life, God. He will insure that you individually will be a part of His life. He loves you for who you are right now. Accept Him for who is, The Great I Am. Man lies and say they are the creator, and many are deceived. When you accept Him as your Savoir deception flees.

Jan 12th everyday start with Jesus, thank Him for the things that happened yesterday. It will remind you of who is the creator and that he is with you always. Good, bad, or indifferent He has brought you through another day. He said He would never leave you or forsake you. He is with you for this life and the life you will have with Him on that street paved in Gold. He is with you forever

Jan 11th every day that you need a boost, a boost of any kind, just ask and you will receive. Doubt is something that belongs to us. The Israelites just caused a dry sea, yet a few days later they wailed about no food. Don't worry He will provide all your needs He said this in his word many,

many times. Love Him for who He is, His love for you provided you with a Savoir through His son Jesus, and a piece of them both through His Spirit. Don't doubt

Jan 10th His word seems to most to be a mystery, but there is a key to understanding His written word the Bible. Man, doesn't hold that key. You can obtain this key in one way, submission to the Trinity. When you do this the Holy Spirit, the very Spirit of Jesus will began unlocking mysteries that are impossible for man to conceive. It all began on the Cross, and our separation from our Lord also ended there through His only begotten Son Jesus. Submit to Him and begin life anew

Jan 9th Wake up with His praises on your mind, thanks for what God has done and created, love for His Son Jesus who went through the valley of death and conquered it so He can escort us through it every day. Don't ask yourself has Jesus been here before because the answer is yes

Jan 8th God has chosen a path for His children, that path is written very clearly in His word, the bible. He has given us a redeemer in His very own Son Jesus. He has given us a guide in His Spirit, and mapped out the road from the world to eternity. Nothing is hidden, why do many fail. They fail because they believe in the created more than the Creator

Jan 7th who do you trust to run your life, the world takes, takes, and takes. The people of this world take, take, and take. These are the sons of Belial that have nothing to give. The Lord gave His only begotten Son to insure you could leave this world of take, He only had one Begotten Son and He sent Him to redeem, save, love, love, teach, comfort, and to give His life for you and me

Jan 6th wake up with a smile and praise God, He has never left your side, He knows your goals and He is with you. He knows your needs and He provides them. He knows your wants, desires, aspirations, there is nothing He does not know about you, and He is for you. His love for you motivates His every thought. You are His purpose

Jan 5th where do we go from here, straight to our knees? praise God for who He is, praise Jesus for who He is the one who created everything you will ever see is also the one who created our Redeemer Jesus. Our creator never created anything bad, the created however turned creation bad. Turn back through Jesus and reclaim victory, victory in Jesus

Jan 4th have you giving your burdens to Him, Jesus said He would carry them for us. Jesus has stated many times of His love for us, our problem is we don't think we are worthy, He does not care how soiled or damaged you are, He will send everything we need to clean us up, Jesus deals in damaged goods and makes them better than they were. Accept Him, He has already accepted you

Jan 3rd so many things on our minds, we are going to do this, we are going to do that. another thing that we attempt on our own and fail. nothing is possible with man, all is possible with Jesus, He said this. He will not fail us, He said this, just two of the wonderful commitments that He said will be yours through Him. He does not lie, He said this. Truly what better friend can you have than Jesus

God Made You

Jan 2nd God is on my mind, His Spirit speaks to us when we wake up in the morning, after His Spirit has watched over us all night. Listen, His words should be the first words we hear when we awake, and they will be if you listen. God is guiding us and talking to us always. If you don't hear Him guess who is not listening. Ignore Him and ignore Eternity

Jan 1st Do not wake up this morning promising yourself that I am going to change, the only change that you can assure is going to happen is when you accept Jesus as your Savoir and King. He knows what is around the corner, he knew before the corner was created. He has given you a part of Himself to help you in this walk we call life, and He calls a blink of the eye. That is His Spirit, and His Sprit will guide you

Dec 31st Make a change today, wake up prepared to serve others when needed or asked, look for opportunities to serve. Jesus was born on this earth and He said I am here to serve, that was an example for us. Along with accepting Jesus is also accepting His examples in how to conduct our own life's, so just accept His wonderful and grace filled name, accept his wonderful and grace filled way of life

Dec 30th Man has no Idea what in the world what his actions produce, he does not know the future. Accept Jesus and your eyes will begin to see reality as it really is, his spirit will guide you to a future that is sure and true, because He knows it. Be assured, have no doubt, He is King

Dec 29th Good your awake, forget about numero uno and pause to reflect on the real number one, God the creator of everything including your salvation. Before Jesus was proclaimed your King, He insured your salvation. He didn't go through what he did to watch you throw it away. He has already given this to you, except Jesus and proclaim your salvation

Dec 28th God is still looking for you to respond to Him. He knows where you are at always, because He is always watching out for you. The question is not why is God still waiting on you, the question is why do you think you are the one waiting on Him. You will never be in front of God, you may not be behind Him either. Our creator loves you get beside him and fell His love for you

Dec 27th, it is a new day, what has changed. Nothing, you are still loved by our lord and savior Jesus, the son of the creator of everything you will ever see in your life, including the reflection in your mirror. His love for you is the number one thing in His life, make Him the number one thig in your life

Dec 26th, He is still King, Jesus is King. Man, would want you to think He is a fairy tale, and the world agrees with what man says. He told pontius that His kingdom was not of this world, if His kingdom was of this world His servants would fight for Him. Fight for Him Christian, don't just watch as the world religions tell the world their gods are real. profess the name of Jesus and He will profess your name to our Father

Dec 25th Christmas is here, next is New Year's day with its resolutions here is one, if you haven't sought out the King, our Lord and Savior Jesus , resolve to do that, seek out the Fathers word every day, ask for His guidance first, He will help you with His Spirit and His Word. The choice is yours, I pray you seek Him first

Dec 24th, we don't know when Jesus was born, but I can assure you that He was born, He was born to bear our transgressions, Accept Him and be reborn again. Commit your life to Him and a wonderful connection with the Father will once again be present, the same connection Adam felt before his transgression. Accept Jesus as your Lord and Savior and be reborn.

Dec 23rd what's on your Christmas list, If you don't know Jesus surely all your gifts are worldly, but Jesus has said He has gifts for you also. The problem is His gifts do not mix with those of the world, His are spiritual gifts. These gifts are not under a tree or delivered by santa, His gifts are personally delivered by our Lord and Savior Jesus. The first gift He will give you is a new birth, and after that they continue all the way to the end of eternity

Dec 22nd, you will not find Him unless you are looking for Him, don't open yourself to the spiritual world without seeking the Father or the Son by name, Jesus I ask for your guidance in my life today, tomorrow, and forever, He wants to hear from you daily, He has prepared a way for you, He knows the way so follow Him to eternity

Dec 21st where do we start when we don't know where to start, we start in prayer and praise to our Father, Jesus told us this as He taught us. His light will illuminate our future. Start with the Alpha and Omega, the beginning and the end and you will never be lost

God Made You

Dec 20th refresh and revive yourself, drink deeply from the well of living water our wonderful Lord and Savior Jesus Christ has provided for our renewal, He gives it to us freely and it is full to the brim with His love for us

Dec 19th, He gave me rest, and he longs to give all of us rest, give your burdens to Jesus and He will lighten your load. He didn't do all the things He did and suffer through all the pain He endured to tell you no, He is always knocking trust in Him and His Father Amen

Dec 18th The truth will set you free, and, the Truth will set you free, Jesus knows who you are, you need not try to hide the real you, guess what, He wants you just the way you are, He will mend you and He starts from the inside not the outside, Jesus loves your morning face, He knows you without make up and He loves you, as your relationship grows in Him and through Him your heart will begin to glow giving you a radiance that can be seen on the outside, a Jesus radiance, a Holy Ghost radiance, a God radiance, people will ask and you will reply, Jesus Christ, you will truly learn why Jesus is the Way, why Jesus is the Truth, and why Jesus is the Life

Dec 17th Relax and know that Jesus is in charge, He will guide you, He will bless you, He will love you, just the way you are, if you accept Him, Jesus wants you to open the door, but, you have to open the door, when you let Him in blessings will begin to multiply in your life, Jesus will not force anything on you, you must first be willing, Jesus is already willing

Dec 16th The yoke of this world is heavy and burdensome, ease the weight, Jesus said give your worries to Him, He will carry them for you, His yoke is light, Jesus Christ has already conquered this world, Jesus Christ has already conquered death, Jesus said He is the Way, Truth, and Life, these things are under His submission, Jesus will bless you through His Father, our Creator, call out to Jesus today, right now, let Him shower you with Love

Dec 15th Do you need strength today, get it from the only true source, get it from Jesus, He has already been there, He knows the Way, He can be relied on for all your needs, Jesus Christ will bless you if you only ask you will receive, He holds the key, He is the Corner Stone, look toward Jesus in everything, trust in Him, always, He is the only Way

Dec 14th To know Him is to love Him, as you journey through life and find Jesus you have found a companion for eternity, a Friend who intervenes on your behalf to the benevolence of God, our Father who art in Heaven, with Jesus you cannot lose, you will not find your way but His

Way, His path is straight and narrow but He will guide you, the Lord of Lords, King of Kings will never leave you, if you think you are lost He is waiting, a love above all love

Dec 13th Involve Jesus in everything you do, let Him guide you, He only wants the best for you, the better decision is His not yours, the better decision is His not the worlds, the better decision is His not the father of lies, Jesus Christ love for you is so deep and endearing, He always will lead you to the best outcome for you in any situation you find yourself in, Trust in Jesus because He is Trustworthy

Dec 12th Start today starting with God, not just with him on your mind but as though He is your very reason for existing, He created you to exist with Him not to exist without Him

Dec 11th let's not dwell on the unknown anymore, know the King, know His word. Our God is not a God of confusion, seek the answers through his Spirit and they will be answered, look deeply and all will be revealed. God said test the spirits(and you will see any deception that is coming from the enemy)

Dec 10th why do we search for answers that have already been answered, and these answers cannot be improved upon. if you cannot find the answer you are looking for, you are looking in all the wrong places. it is simple open the book of answers we call the bible, not a bible written by men for men, but the Bible God , Jesus, and the Holy Ghost wrote, inspired, and lived to show His children His Glory

Dec 9th Wake up, with our technological advancements we cannot compare to the Great I Am, don't let anyone fool you what we call ours are really His, they have been since the beginning of time. Man, will deceive you and claim glory, but his glory is only a spark compared to the Son

Dec 8th My prayer is we all seek God in what we say and do today, He said seek my face and you will find me. If anyone is hiding it is us. God cannot and will not hide his glory, I know in the end we will not be able to find Him, that is because we will quit looking not because He is not there, find Him now and you will never be separated from Him, if you wait till the end to search it is you that are looking to late

Dec 7th Where do we start today, God said He was the Alpha and Omega, the Beginning and the End. Don't try to figure out where to start when Jesus and the Father have already told all of us to start with Him. Our problem is we are searching for answers that have already been provided, the Great I Am is where we start

Dec 6th what are you waiting on, the invitation has been given, except your Kings salvation and grace, if you are lacking it is not because He has not begged for you , it is because you have not excepted, except and live with Him forever starting now, or deny Him and He will except your choice and deny you to the Creator

Dec 5th, you may have to guess what man's next move is going to be, you will never have to guess what our Lord's next move will be, He has hidden nothing from our view, as a matter of fact He has provided us with his own Spirit to remind us if we began to forget. He loves us and wants us with Him for eternity

Dec 4th Our work week is over but our Lords never ends, his priority is you, He will never fail you, He will never stop knocking, and once you open that door your life will change forever as you relish the love he has for you

Dec 3rd He is here, and He is reaching out to help you , let Him in your heart and all will begin to mend, health , relationships , everything that has a real importance in your life, everything will begin anew and you will magnify his wonderful love and grace within yourself, His love is agape

Dec 2nd don't wake up this morning thinking what kind of day is ahead, remember that you are a child of God, all you have to do is ask to receive, all you have to do is look to see, your walk is protected because your walk is with God

Dec 1st Jesus provides everything and He knows when, where, and how much is needed every and all times a need arises, He monitors all events that his servants are in and with love provides

Nov 30th Think of today as another opportunity to spread the Gospel of Jesus , that is your purpose. If you are committed to Jesus than his love will shine through you, His grace will be your grace. Nothing is impossible if Jesus is in the picture

God Made You

Nov 29th Days are rough, hold on to Jesus, and He will hold onto you, initiate this relationship and all of life's worries will vanish as the glory and grace of Jesus takes precedence in your life, yes Jesus is the answer

Nov 28th do not give up on your walk with Jesus, things may seem hard today, build your strength through Him and the Holy Spirit he has given to you so you can endure . His name in itself is so powerful, know who you belong to, He will not forsake you

Nov 27th why do anything remarkable today, because fellowship with other Christians enhances our abilities for worship to a God that is all loving, demonstrate to the world who you are, Jesus knows but he has asked that we bring others into the fold, let the world know you are a follower of Jesus you are a Christian, He said if you are ashamed of Him He will be ashamed of you

Nov 26th Jesus is watching you, he has been watching and waiting for an invitation into your heart, He can't stand you thinking you are alone, He keeps you safe and you won't acknowledge it is Him. Open your heart and drink from the water that you never thirst again for, because He will never leave you

Nov 25th the day after and the world changed, how do you keep up with this constant change. Ask Jesus to change your heart once and forever, after this you don't have to worry how many times the world changes, you have gave your life over to the one true constant, Jesus

Nov 24th who should we be thankful for today, what should we be thankful for today, the answer is Jesus and

God Made You

the what is the love he has for all of us, who made the choice to die in our place He did. He did it because the Father asked it of Him Ask and you will receive

Nov 23rd Jesus will give us gifts when we see each other face to face, we will be so struck with his glory that we will simple lay them back at his feet as we praise Him for his very existence, the glory, the beauty, we will be awestruck when we look upon His continence

Nov 22nd what can I say, nothing, all has been promised to us by our Savoir Jesus, the only begotten Son of God. He gave us a complete example of life, and waits with rewards for those of us that love him

Nov 21st where are you this morning, still in bed, awake, it doesn't matter He is with you where ever you are He waits silently for you, talk to Him and watch in amazement as the blessings begin to flow as he talks with you

Nov 20th Our Lord and Savior has something waiting for you in Paradise, He has already shown you what he is willing to do for you, what are you willing to do for him, there is nothing you can do receive what He has for you unless you accept him as your Lord and Savoir

Nov 19th that is why He left His glorious home called Heaven, to serve you, He stopped to serve and show us the truth of love and caring for one another, serve each other as he served us, in doing so we will see a little bit of eternal love

Nov 18th, we celebrate so much, when there is only one event to really celebrate, what God has promised for those that love him is greater than any birthday in the past, His rebirth is our rebirth, our total rebirth ends up with Him

Nov17th **Don't let the world fool you, all that you see was created and is testament to the Creator, yes the world was created by our Father who is in Heaven, there was no big bang or any other reason, our existence is solely the responsibility of the Creator, God has even given us a Way back to Him through His only Begotten Son Jesus Christ, and He is the only Way back, sin changed everything, Jesus Christ changed it back, accept Him as Lord and Savior, and return to the graces and blessings that you are created to have**

Nov 16th, we look all over for the answer, we try to find something where there is nothing, look toward Jesus and you will find the answer, look toward Jesus and you will find everything

Nov 15th Oh what we as children of God have in store, He loves us so much that he has a longing to take all our pains away, all our tears, we will only have one emotion, and we will truly love our neighbors as our selves

Nov 13th God loves all of us, here is one of the mysteries of the marriage of the Lamb, He means it when he says for eternity, His love for you will never die, it's one thing you have now and will never lose, can't lose, because Jesus holds it

God Made You

Nov 12th today is day that the Lord has made, so was yesterday, and so will tomorrow, always present , always involved, always loving, always caring, Jesus is always with you, you cannot outrun his love no matter how long you try just like the one lost sheep He is coming for you

Nov 11th wake up this morning with Jesus, and share his Glory and Grace as you Greet everyone you meet, do the three Gs for Jesus

Nov 10th Looks like here in this world there are exceptions for everything, if you want to be sure of your destination look toward Jesus, look toward God, He provides the one true way, He provides the only way, and He loves you is the best part of all. Make your destination an eternal bliss with Him

Nov 9th, we have a new president but the path is not his, the path was chosen by our God and Lord and Savior Jesus, His will be done He has answered prayer, Our Nation is one under God

Nov 8th, I will not initially write when I awake in the morning because I do not want a clue, remember that we are voting for a president, we have chosen a King, and that King whose name is Jesus will lead us from here to eternity, the Pres is good for 4 at best 8 years, stay with the King God has provided for us

Nov 8th Many of us are wondering what today will bring, whatever it is remember God is in control, his will be done, He will watch over his children, his children will survive, His love is never ending

God Made You

Nov 7th Don't bend to the world, pray that you are strengthened with His strength, a strength that does not fail. The world bends and molds itself to conform to sin, His path is straight and a jot to walk

Nov 6th, We may not know what time it is but God knows, all seeing, all hearing, all tasting, all touching, all smelling, He was there before you, you cannot travel were He has not been, knowing everything He loves you with more love than all your senses can imagine

Nov 5th The wonderful thing is, you don't have to look, Jesus is already there, you don't have to wonder, Jesus is already waiting, you don't have to guess, Jesus already knows, seek and you will find , ask and you will receive

Nov 4th everything that happens in life, is to bring you closer to the Father, there will be a reunion someday, and by grace it will be beautiful, point blank God misses you

Nov 3rd The Father cannot tell a lie yet we find it hard to believe all his grace, what He does on a daily basis , open your eyes and revel in the delights that see, hear ,taste, touch, and smell, all is provided by Him for you, it is not automatic, it is a blessing from Him to you, every day he does not forget

Nov 2nd what can I tell you about Him, He has a love for you which we cannot understand, undying and unending. He wants to be a part of your life and the more we know no of him, the less we want to know of ourselves. Know Him and his love will consume you

Nov 1st, we too often celebrate things which are of this world only, celebrate the creator not the created, He is so much more than what we can see with our naked eye. You can see and hear Him just listen

Oct 31st As you wake up this morning look around and know all of this is going to give way to a new heaven and a new earth, God has told us this in his word, a new heaven and a new earth are coming, They are permanent and God will be there with us

Oct 28th Look and you will find the Lord, He is not hiding, if you are having trouble finding Him Humble yourself, He is King not you

Oct 27th The question is not where is God the question is where are you, His love is so much that he has no choice but to be beside you forever waiting for you to say come in, He will never forsake you or leave you alone, can you say the same thing about attitude toward Him

Oct 26th the last supper began a new covenant through Jesus Christ, He gave his life so we could once again have not only a personal relationship with him but also the Father, there is not a better love than His

Oct 25th Look around and you will notice that God is everywhere you have needed him to be and always will His love for you is never ending

Oct 24th Why search your whole life for peace, it can't be found in the world, Jesus said come to me all that are heavy laden, don't let this world pull you down, allow Jesus Christ to pull you up, His burden is light, He has already paid the price for your salvation, His love for you and His Fathers will allows peace in your heart, acceptance is all it takes, Jesus has taken care of everything, the price has been paid by a loving King of Kings, accept Jesus Christ as your Savior today

Oct 23rd So many different names for one creator, why, because he can accomplish every need , every want, and above an eternal life which is beyond imagination

Oct 22nd Don't look at the outside, look on the inside where the Holy Spirit is waiting to guide, teach and comfort. God has provided a guide to eternal salvation and bliss

Oct 21st Wake up with a smile Christian, your life has changed for eternity when you accepted Jesus as your Lord and Savior

Oct 19th Jesus was sent by the Father to intercede on our behalf, he came and left us with the comforter the Holy Ghost, he is with us always, seek and it will be handed to you

Oct 18th unlike us God will never forget you, God always has time for you He will always Love you even when it is the hardest for us to love even ourselves, His love is forever and his mood never changes, He is and always will be waiting for you to return

Oct 17th Get up knowing that Jesus has been watching you sleep waiting for you to awaken so that he can bless you with his love

God Made You

Oct 16th God has not forgotten you, you are the first thing he thinks about, he knocks continuously, never stopping. Is God your first thought in the morning, stop and pray and thank him for who he is.

Oct 15th Guess what, if it is not getting to overbearing for you, God is still in charge and he loves you what better combination could you have in your life. Oh yea he also sent his Son to insure your salvation.

Oct 14th Don't forget about this wonderful love God has for you, a love that only grows each day, a love that never falters, one that only intensifies every second. Ask and you will receive

Oct 13th Our Father has known us from the beginning and his love never faltered even when ours did, he is always thinking of you, he thinks so much of us he sent us a savoir, Jesus

Oct 12th Make God number one in your life and make Jesus number one in your life and blessings will overflow all your expectations

Oct 11th Start your morning with someone who loves you, has always loved you, and will never abandon you, Jesus is always loving and always caring

Oct 10th God is amongst us and he cares, things are for him, he is in charge. Many different entity's want you to believe he doesn't care , he does and you are his #1 thought

Oct 9th Don't look outside for the answer to life, look inside where God has placed his Spirit, he has provided a

God Made You

teacher, comforter, and his love to guide you on a path to eternal life

Oct 8th God is wonderful, and all that he created, but the most beautiful is his son Jesus

Oct 7th God is looking your way always with love and compassion, waiting, knocking, once you give him an invitation he will change your life forever, things that can only be dreamt of without his presence

Oct 6th Don't let you worries blur your vision of him, he is all knowing, all loving, and all caring God will be there before you

Oct 5th God loves us this morning he will love us forever listen 4 Hour Shepherds voice seek and you shall find him

Oct 4th why as the created we try to accomplish the job of the creator
Ask God to secure your salvation for eternity, he has already provided the way, and that way is provided through his only begotten son Jesus Christ

Oct 3rd Wake up this morning knowing that our creator is in charge, and guess what you are one of his number one priorities

Oct 2nd Good Morning, don't just start one day a week with God and Jesus, and the Holy Spirit at the beginning of your things to do , put them first always, everyday

Oct 1st Wake up and greet our king Jesus, the son of God, ask him to guide you and he will, personally, he loves you and me

Sept 29th Let Him guide your way, the path is narrow, He has provided a Comforter, Guide, Teacher, and Every other that you can think of, let Jesus direct your steps, and he will walk you to Glory

Sept 28th Praise Him always Morning, Afternoon, and Night. Let God be your point man, Let Him lead in all thoughts and actions, He will never leave you or forsake you

Sept 27th Jesus has stated that he wants to bless you, his Father has said he wants to bless you, only the creator can do this, none of the created can, open your eyes to his glory and love

Sept 26th What can I say, our God is wonderful, all knowing, all caring, and you are his number one concern, his love is everlasting

Sept 25th wake up glorifying our Father who created all things seen or unseen remember that his love is everlasting, choice is why man does evil not because the Father ordained it

Sept 24th Jesus bought you with his blood, the Father created you, don't be in denial of your heritage, don't let the world deceive you

Sept 23rd God is already waiting on you, he was waiting when you went to sleep, he never stops loving you and wants to bless every step you take

Sept 22nd The one that created you knows your worth, we are the ones that don't, ask him and he will give it to you, seek him and you will find him, He is not hiding from you

God Made You

Sept 21st Rejoice, smile and remember He loves you more than you love period, a love above any love you have ever known or thought you knew

Sept 20th Our King and Savoir Jesus Christ is what's on my mind, start your day with him and blessings will follow

Sept 19th Good Morning, God is still in charge and his Son is still our Lord and Savior and when the smoke clears it will be the same. Nowhere else do your blessings come from

Sept 18th Christians understand that God is in authority, Israel went into captivity for their transgression, but remember he also brought them out of their captivity, turn from other Idols and give your full focus to God and his only begotten son Jesus Christ

Sept 18th Don't worry about the things of this world, such as what just happened in NY, he has a hedge around you, you belong to Him, he bought you for a price

Sept 17th Don't seek comfort through the things of this world, they are only temporary, seek comfort through Jesus Christ, they are permanent and forever, Jesus holds the key to forever, His blessings are everlasting just as His love is everlasting, rely on Jesus for all that is permanent including your life, His gift is free and fully paid for, He is our Savior and Lord, come to Jesus today, just the way you are, and begin life anew

God Made You

Sept 16th Everything you have done or ever will do he has paid for with his blood, love your king and savoir Jesus Christ

Sept 15th Our Father is waiting to bless you and every aspect of your life, through his son Jesus Christ

Sept 14th Good Morning The wonderful thing is God never sleeps, he is always aware of your needs

Sept 13th Good Morning, I know how to make it great, start with God and include him always

Sept 12th Good Morning, let his grace shine through you today, and share his love

Sept 11th, it is Sunday, and Jesus is knocking, open the door he is waiting for an invitation from you. Blessings will abound

Sept 10th Good morning walk with Jesus and start your day in prayer and praise to God

Sept 9th Good Morning, may God enrich your days with his blessings and healing touch

Sept 8th Good Morning, let it begin being a God Morning, start with him first

Sept 7th Good Morning Praise Jesus, he wants to bless you

Sept 6th Good Morning, I have a prayer for you, that is that your day is blessed, and God enriches every step you take

God Made You

Sept 5th Good morning, Jesus and his Father want to bless you, start your day out with them

Sept 4th Good Morning, the lord Jesus Christ is still with us today, and wants to bless you throughout it, ask and you will receive

Sept 3rd Good Morning, may God bless your day, and walk with you throughout it

God Made You

God Made You

God Made You

God Made You

More Devotionals

Sept 3rd There are so many ideas and options to living, man will tell everyone a different solution to life. Here is what I know, there are many ways, but there is only one Way, start with a one-sided conversation with our Lord and Savior Jesus Christ, the one-sided conversation means let Him be in control, give your problems to Him, His yoke is light, begin your day with prayer to our Father which art in Heaven through His only begotten Son Jesus Christ through whom all things have been renewed, be born again, begin your life today anew, and every day anew, begin your day with a prayer

Sept 4th Looking for direction, you don't need to look any further than Jesus Christ, He said I Am the Way, I Am the Truth, I Am the Life, sounds controlling but it isn't Jesus does not give any one more than they can bare, He provides His Holy Spirit to walk with you, to talk with you, Jesus said He will never leave you nor forsake you, He loves us with a love that is never ending, take that first step of acceptance and you will be drawn into a world were all you have is benefits, there are no disadvantages, there is only Truth

Sept 5th Whatever happens there will always be another rainbow, it is a promise from God to every living being, therefore it is Truth. Many trials and tribulations will come before us, God said you will not be burdened with more than you can handle. I think that there is a hidden message of Salvation in those words, Jesus said you can do nothing without Him, yes to survive these burdens you need to accept Jesus Christ, the only begotten Son of God, as your Lord and Savior, He said his burdens are light, He will see you through

Sept 6th I notice there are plenty of examples of prayer, know that no one will be able to say I did not know, everyone sees the beauty of the physical world, know that no one can deny that they have not seen the Creator through creation, and before the return of our Creators Son, Jesus Christ, know that no one will be able to say I did not know, every knee shall bow, every tongue confess that Jesus Christ is Lord, our Father who art in Heaven has given Him this title and His authority comes from above

Sept 7th What is going to happen tomorrow, another riot, another storm, another what, are you prepared and will you survive, will you be alive tomorrow, God said worry about today, tomorrow is tomorrow and you can do nothing, you can do nothing without Him. Jesus Christ insures tomorrows always comes, your link to survival is the Trinity of God, His only begotten Son Jesus, and the Holy Spirit, without them there is no use worrying about tomorrow, today, or for that matter any day, when you accept Jesus Christ you accept insurance that you have a mansion in your future, and love for eternity

Sept 8th God is in charge, and yes, He can stir or even stop a storm, all His decisions are True and bring about a better solution than man or angel could ever contemplate. Whatever happens in life there is an outcome of grace in the end. Man will try to distort reality to bend it to their cause but look for Gods vision, not man's division. Understand that God is love, He has given you a personal guide for life through His Son, through His Holy Spirit, and through His word, if you are lost it is because that is your choice.

Sept 9th The disciples thought they were going to drown in a sea of turmoil, what was Jesus doing, sleeping, until they awoke Him and said save us, ye of little faith and He rebuked the sea and the sea became calm. If you have Jesus in your life expect the assurances He provides, these provisions He gives freely, ask and you will receive He holds nothing back, trust in Him no matter the situation, trust in Him no matter what storm life brings your way, easy for you to say when there is no storm on the way, will there is and Jesus will watch over what belongs to Him, and I am happy to say I belong to Him

Sept 10th Well we sit here and wait, uncertain of the future, or not. For those that have accepted Jesus Christ as Savior, King, and Lord, we have a future that is paved in gold, remember Jesus said He will not forsake you or leave you, so remember as you hunker down for this storm and all life's storms He is with you and He said if I am for you who can be against you, the answer is nothing or no body. No trial, including this one, will you be subjected to that Jesus has not conquered, no temptation that may come your way has not been seen and felt by Jesus already. He has already conquered the storm on the sea of galilee as recorded in the written word of the Lord mark 4;37 and He conquered the storm of death also recorded in our Lords living word, bottom line Jesus loves you, you belong to Him

Sept 11th God is still in the blessing business, and He is still in the prayer answering business, God is miraculously still alive, He is the Alpha and Omega, the Beginning and the End. Little troubles and headaches but if you look toward Jesus they all are resolved, He provides to those that ask, if you need a prayer answered it will be, ask and you shall receive, have no doubt that Jesus is Lord of both the seen and unseen, praise Jesus and praise our Father who art in Heaven

Sept 12th It is time to clean up, outwardly everything will look as if nothing happened, inwardly all the debris of life are hidden from view, all that hurt is there, you don't have to carry pain by yourself, give it to Jesus, you are not alone once you become part of His kingdom, all your pains become His pains, all your hurts become His hurts, He has lived all the lies that life hits us with, He conquered them with Truth, He became a King through His ordeals, He became a Savior because of all your sins, He overcame

Hate with love, and that love carried Him through back to the Father, Jesus knows the way because He is the Way

Sept 13th Distractions are everywhere, it seems that you must concentrate whenever you try to accomplish anything worthwhile, stop, and focus your attention on reality. There are many ways to die a second death, so many it takes no conscious effort to achieve it, but not to die a second death has but one solution, turn your eyes to Jesus, turn your thoughts to the only begotten Son of our Father in Heaven, Jesus is the Way, the Truth , and the Life, concentrate on Him and you find that He does not forsake you or leave you, wake up to the reality of Jesus Christ and you find that life takes on a real meaning instead of a road map that has no ending

Sept 14th This is happening, that is happening, this is why, that is why, everyone has an opinion, everyone has a different answer, why not look where the True answers are already recorded, look to the living word of God, all the answers to all the questions are recorded in the bible. God said these things will happen, no one has to guess, God even provides a solution to all woes of this earth, that solution did not originate on earth but in Heaven, that solution is Jesus Christ, He has all the answers, and loves us enough to share them with us, He is the expert, He is the solution, He is our Lord, Savior, King, and He will return

Sept 15th Your King is coming, many people deny His grace and glory, many people claim it is a false hope, many people will die a final death that there is no returning from. The living word of God says do not take part in the second death, this death is permanent and eternity is forever, your chance to skip this judgement is to accept the One who has already paid the price for sin, the One that will never leave you, nor forsake you, claim victory in this life by turning to the Son of God, the only begotten Son Jesus Christ, your advocate to redemption, redemption is yours, no longer do you need to Hope your Salvation is secure, with Jesus it is finished, He is all truth, He is the King both physically and spiritually, He is the answer to life

Sept 16th Mankind cannot accomplish anything without the blessing of the only true God, a God that was not created by man, but a God who created man. Man has knowledge, but without the wisdom of God, will only use that knowledge for naught, seek guidance from our Creator and your endeavors will be fruitful, however to reach the Father you must go through the Son, Jesus Christ is the only conduit to the Father. Seek Jesus as your personal Savior, accept Jesus as Lord, please the Father through the Son, the price has been paid in full by Jesus Christ, man has nothing he can do but accept the Redeeming power of the Last Sacrifice, the blood of Jesus Christ, the only begotten Son of God

Sept 17th Are the words of God too hard to understand, or do they give man a sense of moral guidance which impedes his inner nature, we cannot understand the words of God if we do not understand the words of His Son Jesus Christ, Gods word says no one goes to the Father but through the Son, so to understand Gods written word understand and then accept the sacrifices of the Son, there is only one Way, there is only one Truth, there is only one Life. Don't let man deceive you, don't let the devil deceive you, don't let the world deceive you, there is no direction in a lie

Sept 18th As you walk with the Lord you will notice that you are given more and more of His attributes, you will begin to apply His actions of love in your life, and thoughts will start to become positive instead of negative, Jesus gives more than Life, He gives love and that love develops more and more in you as you walk with Him, there are no negatives in accepting Jesus Christ as your Lord and Savior, only positives, So many people are blind to His Grace and Glory, so many people are lost to this world, if you know Jesus Christ share who He is with those that do not know Him, plant a seed, you may or may not see it grow, but you have taken part in the great commission

Sept 19th The power of The Alpha and Omega, yet so many turn to something created such as the world, or satan himself, instead of our one true and only God, from the beginning God the Father knew everything, from the beginning Jesus His Son knew everything and they still created, why because They already loved you, They always knew there would be a remnant that belonged to

Them, that longed for fellowship with our Creators, and yes the Father, the Son, and the Holy Spirit took part in creation, so many think they are equal, some sects claim they are on an equal footing with God, the Beginning and the End, moses saw His glory from behind and wore a veil the rest of His life because his face was outwardly aglow, accept Jesus Christ and you will begin to glow from the inside and as your fellowship with Him continues people will even notice the glow from outside, the glow of His tremendous love that has been present from the beginning

Sept 20th Everything you ever needed is yours for the asking, everything you need, not want. Jesus said He would never leave you or forsake you, in other words He will never forget you because of the love He has for you, it doesn't matter what you were before you came to Him, He will make you anew, for you to truly repent is for Him to truly forgive, in Him, and through Him you are born again and life with Him is life eternal. Jesus Christ is the only begotten Son of God, He paid a price you could not and freely gives salvation

Sept 21st Do you know what the function of your spiritual heart is, without a relationship with Jesus Christ it is impossible, He is the way, He is the only way. Without Jesus you will never know what you are capable of, without Jesus you are not complete, your body, soul, and spirit are not compatible, and you will stay lost to the reality of who you really are and what agape love is, reach your full potential, bring the spiritual part of you together with the physical part, accept Jesus Christ as your Savior and King, and live for Him in so doing you live also for the Father, our Creator, and Only True God

Sept 22nd Why is the world the way it is, so many protest, so many wars, so many rights turned to wrongs and vis versa, because Jesus has not returned yet, our King and Savior comes to subdue the nations, the Bible, the word of God proclaims that Jesus will, and His will be done. People can deny the Truth until people run head long into the Truth, and that time will be too late, accept the only begotten Son of God now, accept Jesus now, secure your eternal future now, the bible says that there will be a new Heaven and a new earth, it does not say there will be a new God or new Son of God, so prepare yourself for eternity, establish a relationship with Jesus and receive a heart of flesh, and learn the love the Trinity has for you

Sept 23rd Where are you today, accepting the day to day turmoil of the world and thinking you must accept it, you have no choice? You have a choice, that choice was given to you freely on a tree on Golgotha, what happened there , a price was paid for you, a price you could not pay, Jesus died for the sins of the world, His death was the final sacrifice, He gave you a choice, that choice is to accept Him or accept the world, the choice is to live for an eternity with God and His only begotten Son Jesus, or dying for an eternity in the bottomless pit of agony with satan and the fallen angels in the absence of your creator, your choice, you make it, gain redemption through Jesus, our Lord and Savior, or spend eternity imprisoned with the father of lies, who has no redeeming powers, and can never set you free

Sept 24th Are you committed to God, you cannot be if you have not committed to His Son, if you think you can reach eternity without Jesus Christ, you are mistaken? The father of lies would have you believe that being a good person, and basically following a few laws will get you to heaven, these actions will not. You have to accept Jesus as your Lord, your Savior, and your Redeemer, no one goes to the Father alone, you must have his Son Jesus Christ with you to enter the graces of His Father, no works that we do will, only by faith in Jesus will you enter, commit to Jesus today and the real meaning of life will be revealed to you

Sept 25th Stand up for Jesus, look around you at creation, man was not involved in creation, as a matter of fact he was created last, everyone has an agenda over everything and anything but praise for the Creator, praise the Creator, find His Son Jesus and you will start a new agenda of loving your neighbors instead of hate. In Jesus you will find what you are looking for, accept Jesus and receive crowns, accept man and receive hate, in the end every knee will bow and every tongue confess that Jesus Christ is Lord, not might, will, you gain a winning situation in Jesus, you receive a losing proposition in man, accept Jesus Christ as your personal Savior and Lord

Sept 26th Everyone has their own opinions and whether they are a lie or not try to push them to the front, Jesus doesn't give an opinion, He gives truth, and it is free for the asking, you won't find His gift casually sitting around by its own, this gift is way too large to leave unattended, this gift which Jesus holds cannot be duplicated, although many attempt to sale imposters, this gift is Jesus Christ Himself, the only begotten Son of our God, He is a key to a continued relationship with our Heavenly Father, He is the gift of Salvation, don't accept a counterfeit that has no redeeming power, understand fully who Jesus is, He is the Way, the Truth, and the Life

Sept 27th Why can't people see the proof that is all around them, everyone that has at least one of the senses knows that creation is everywhere in their day to day travels, creation testifies that there is a Creator, a one true God, and our God gives you wisdom through His word on the Beginning and the End, even to tell of the past, present, and future, and tells of His relationship and our relationship with His only begotten Son Jesus Christ and how that relationship frees us from a second death that ends up in a place that is forever lost to this relationship with the Trinity, how can people deny they did not know, they can't establish that relationship today, start with Jesus and so doing finish with Jesus

Sept 28th Our God wants you to seek Him out, He wants you to know that you can rely on Him, if only you would ask, but so many people do not until life is in turmoil and the path to God is clouded and unclear, do this now, accept Gods Son Jesus Christ as your Lord and Savior, this is just two of His many names, another is Intercessor, He is the only way of reaching the Creator, our God and Lord, the only way. You may be dying but there is only one way, Jesus said no one goes to the Father except through Him, the three agree, the Father, the Son, and the Holy Ghost, the problem is you need to agree with Them, accept Jesus today

Sept 29th, It seems a lot of people think they do not need a Shepard, they will continue wandering aimlessly around trying to find support, they will often return to places in their life where they think they have found a temporary pasture, they often remain lost and have no direction. Jesus Christ is the Good Shepard, He will take you to good pastures, He will lay you down by still waters, He will never forsake you nor leave you, He will protect you with His life, the grass is greener on His side of the fence, He is gracious and will accept you into His fold, all you have to do is accept Him, it will cost you nothing He has already paid the price and has freed you to walk with Him, He loves you , come to Him and find green pasture

Sept 30th In the face of adversity do not lose your faith in Jesus Christ, reassure your faith in Jesus Christ, hardship will hit both the good and the evil, both the believer and the non-believer, there is one thing that the believer has that a non-believer doesn't have, a relationship with a Creator that loves them, when adversity hits draw closer to your Lord and Savior Jesus Christ, rest in His assurance not the lies of satan, once you believe in your Redeemer your eternity is secure, you are saved and no longer lost, attacks from the adversary increase as your love for Jesus increases, attacks from the adversary increase when your love for your neighbor increases, attacks from the adversary increase when you become more like Jesus and less like him

Oct 1st, You can change your opinion, you are allowed to make a mistake, you are allowed to change the direction you are going, you can walk a different path in life. Jesus Christ's love for you has given you these opportunities, He has already paid for every mistake, every sin, and every wayward direction you take, His love for you insures you a Way back to our Father in Heaven, you can be wrong and still find your Way in and through Jesus, what Jesus went through was done for His Father and it was done for you, He has paid the price, salvation is free to you, nothing you do will insure this, only Jesus, if you haven't found Him, find Him now

Oct 2nd The devil needs permission to attack, man does not, a man without a cause will look for a cause, a civilized man is only a misconception away from anarchy. There is only one place to find secure footing and that is with the living Word of God, His Son Jesus Christ, it is not a fanatical religion, it is a fanatical relationship only full of love, the name Christian does not reflect this relationship, Jesus, the only begotten Son of God our Father, reflects this relationship, Jesus is the Head of this relationship, not the created, Jesus reflects Himself through the Holy Spirit He guides you with, your right, you cannot do it by yourself, seek Jesus, inherit eternity

Oct 3rd When we are lost for words as to why something happened don't look toward God look toward man. If you want to know why something happened look Oct 4th toward the written word of God, the bible tells us of the things on earth that will begin to happen, Adam was cast out of Eden, and shortly after love diminished, and man began to attempt to survive without God, and cain killed abel. Man cannot replace God with anything man creates, there is only one Way back to the Way it should be, that Way is reliance on Him that God sent, not him that God cast out, God sent Jesus, God cast out satan and man. Jesus is the only Way, Jesus is the only Truth, and Jesus is the only Life, no one goes to the Father but through the Son

Oct 5th Stop wondering what today and tomorrow hold, anything that can be done has already been done, you don't have to wait for the outcome, the outcome has already been prepared, it is preordained by our Creator, oh, there is one thing that can be done, accept the gift of the Holy Spirit, receive this gift by accepting another gift given to you by our Father who art in Heaven, and that's the gift of His Son Jesus Christ, and by accepting this free gift you receive another free gift of a pardon from all the offenses against God that you will ever do. Jesus paid a price we could not and gives it freely to those that ask, regain a relationship with God through His only begotten Son

Oct 6th I don't have answers that are mine to how life unfolds, however you can find the answers in Gods living word, I can't tell you were to go to find solstice, but Jesus can, I cannot be by your side all day but the Holy Spirit can, Jesus said He would never leave you , nor forsake you, when you accept Jesus He becomes part of you ,to help you, to guide you, to lead you, however He will not demand that you follow Him, He will not force you to walk in His footsteps, He will give you all these things freely, but you must accept freely, you will find that His love for you is so powerful that you will choose to follow Him, you will find that He is the Way. Nothing is forced upon you, all is given to you freely in and through Jesus Christ

Oct 7th For those of you that are unsure, Jesus is still waiting, for those of you that are still lost, open the door, Jesus is knocking, for those of you that are waiting for an invitation, Jesus gave that invitation over 2000 years ago, Jesus is not the one that needs to decide, it is you. Jesus, the only begotten Son of God, decided, His decision was to do the will of the Father, and His decision will set you free, free to bask in the glory of the Father, Jesus paid the price for your redemption, it cost you nothing but a decision, a decision to follow Jesus instead of the world, look to Jesus for your salvation, He is the only source

Oct 8th Can you explain your actions, why you did or did not do something, because you wanted to? Because you felt like it? You don't know why, maybe it is because you have no guidance in your life, and maybe you don't want any, but if you do there is only one sure source to find guidance, that is the written word of God, oh the answer is not in the bible, you say, it is. I don't have the time to read the bible, you had time to go out with your friends, make time. Nowhere else will you find all truths and no lies, the Bible is one of the stepping stones to eternity, the beginning of a walk that takes you to a mansion, to a Savior who came from the throne room of God to pay a price you could not, to a guide to help in times of indecision and pressure from the world, to the Father, Son, and Holy Ghost

Oct 9th, We have physical hurts and pains, and we ask why, Job asked why, in the end he was restored, God restored Him, this was before Jesus, and yes you can ask why also, Jesus Christ will restore you also, He will personally carry your prayers to the Father and you will be restored, with Him all is possible, without Him nothing is possible. satan will deceive you and momentarily you will think you are restored, Jesus restoration is forever, the devil will falsely accuse you, Jesus is all truth and He will defend you. Nothing is ever just physical it is also spiritual, and our Restorer has dominion over both, Jesus is the answer no matter the circumstances

Oct 10th Does Jesus count, do you use Him as a first thought or a last thought, what comes to mind first, what you are going to do, or who is going to watch you do it, and do you care who sees you do whatever it is you have decided to do. It is not what would Jesus do, it is would you let Jesus watch what you are doing, well guess what He already knows, He is all seeing and all knowing, even all of this did not stop Him from paying for each sin you have or will commit, a price you could not pay. The price will be paid, either you accept Jesus as your Lord and Savior, and in so doing become debt free and sin free, or, pay the price yourself, but a price will be paid

Oct 11th Do you know God, He draws you to Him through His Son Jesus Christ, His word tells us of His Son, His word tells us what His Son did for us when He was crucified, His word tells us that Jesus conquered death, His word tells us that Jesus was resurrected and now sits at the right hand of the Father, His word tells us that Jesus intervenes on the behalf of those that accept Him as their Lord and Savior to His Father who is in Heaven, because of all this Heaven is awaiting the arrival of those that have found the Redeemer God sent from Heaven, so if you know Jesus rejoice, and praise the Father and the Son

Oct 12th Biblical truths are everywhere but some people remain blind to them, some give facts leeway to accommodate lies, twisting and manipulating Gods words into miss- leading ideas, some twist and turn, leave out, or forsake Gods word, how are you to know the truth, Jesus is the Truth, accept Him and accept what comes with Him, the Holy Spirit that will guide you, teach, and lead you to Salvation, Redemption, and Forgiveness. No one goes to the Father but through the Son, no man can interpret the word of God, the only source for wisdom is the Son of God, Jesus Christ

Oct 13th Don't let this world deceive you, don't let satan deceive you, don't let man deceive you, there is only one Way, Jesus Christ is that Way, Jesus said many will claim they are the Messiah they are not, Jesus said many will come in His name they do not. The Truth is in God's word and Jesus is in God's word, Jesus is the Truth, the world does not lead to life, Jesus is the Life, He is the Way back to the Father, He is Life. Man's religions are just that man's, acceptance OF Jesus establishes a relationship with Abba, Father our Creator, Jesus is the street that is straight and narrow, He is our Guide to Heaven

Oct 14th, It is not hard, just turn to Jesus, accept Him as your Lord and Savior, and live an eternity pain free and loved forever. Nothing on earth will give you this, nothing under the earth will give you this, only our Father above in Heaven provides this, and really when you let His Son into your life you will find that you have a different opinion on life, why because you are changed, you are born again through Jesus Christ, the old you fades away and you become a new person in Christ, His wisdom and love began to change who we are, we are prepared for an eternity in the presence of our Creator, the one true God, no one goes to the Father but through the Son

Oct 15th What does it mean when people use our Creator and His Son as simple material to make jokes, Father forgive them, they know not what they do. What does it mean when one searches Gods word for one verse to support their agenda, Father forgive them, they know not what they do, what does it mean when people use a created item to worship, Father forgive them, they know not what they do. God is not fractional, Jesus is not fractional, the Holy Spirit is not fractional, on the seventh day God rested after His work was complete, and He said it is good, Jesus when dying on the cross, said it is finished, upon acceptance of Jesus as your Lord you receive all of the Holy Ghost, God does not work in fractions, His Son does not work in fractions, the Holy Spirit does not work in fractions, They work in completeness and with Them you are complete, accept the Truth not a fractional lie

Oct 16th Remember Jesus, start your day with Him, and you will think of Him all day. It is impossible to negotiate the hazards of this world without Him, by the grace of God we make it to His Son, God draws you to Him, it starts with a thought and grows into an eternal relationship that will change your life, life is not meant to run to and fro looking for a relationship that will last a lifetime, it is meant to regain a relationship with our Creator through His Son Jesus that last throughout this life and our next for an eternity, there are many ways to wreck your life, there is only one way to save your life and that is Jesus Christ

Oct 17th Why is it every day we need to be reminded who our Sovereign Lord is, we that forget so easily because the world throws blinders on during His presence, most say they do not see when a miracle happens, they don't see because they don't know, they don't know our Lord and Savior Jesus Christ, in order to see the physical you must know Him, to see spiritual you must know Him, once you know Jesus the blinders the world placed on you will fall to the side, the scales will fall from your eyes just as they did for Paul when he began to know the One he previously persecuted, Jesus gives you a free pardon to salvation, accept Him as your Lord and Savior and begin life anew

Oct 18th Jesus said that there would be deception, and many will be deceived. Open your heart to Jesus and your eyes will be opened to the real motivations of the world, Jesus said that if I Am for you who can be against you, as your heart opens more and more to Jesus your eyes will begin to see the work of the principalities of this world, you will begin to understand the spiritual battles that are waged daily by satan for control of your heart, he does not want you to have a heart of flesh, he wants you oblivious to the world as you walk blindly into the abyss, open your hearts to Jesus Christ and open your eyes to the reality of this world

God Made You

Oct 19th Is it passé to take note of our Gracious and Awesome God, people will comment 100 of times about football and only give a passing glance at Jesus Christ, people need to get their priority's in order, oh, they do have them in order? Very creation attest to the existence of God, and the Word of God attest to His Son Jesus and what He did for us on the cross, yes Sacrifice is also one of His names, just like Rome there are games to keep your mind occupied, look to the written word of God and be occupied with the wisdom of His Word, and learn of His Son Jesus, get your priority's in order, I didn't know will not work, I had the tv on the wrong channel will not work, in the end every knee will bow and every tongue confess Jesus Christ is Lord

Oct 20th Do not think that you can do anything to insure your future, there is life after you leave this body, and that life will continue for eternity, there is a way to insure where eternity is spent, it is as simple as accepting Jesus Christ as your personal Savior or not, He paid a price that you were never able to pay, He took on sin, and He became a sacrifice, the final sacrifice to set you free, free to continue a relationship with our Father in Heaven, through Gods only begotten Son your eternal life is saved and through Him and only Him you will be set free, pursue Him, pursue the Word of God , pursue eternity, an eternity that is meant to be spent in Heaven, a New Heaven and not in a bottomless pit of despair

God Made You

Oct 21st The Lord is my Shepherd, who is your shepherd, you follow someone, someone shows you the way, you are influenced, the problem is the lost can only lead the lost into despair, Jesus said I am the Way, the only Way, there simply is not another, people will mislead you into thinking that another direction is better, people are influenced by principalities to lead those that do not know the very words of God the Father and Jesus the Son, which are recorded in the Holy Bible, down a path or in a direction that leads to an eternal separation from God, please open His Word and read about the Grace and Love that can be yours

Oct 22nd Where do you come from, why are there different tree's, why is there more than one type of bee, do you really think all this evolved, creation is proof of God, salvation, forgiveness, redemption, love, is proof of His only begotten Son, don't believe me, open your eyes to the very words of God, but remember curiosity killed the cat, and the words of God will change the atheist, seek and you will find, Jesus said I Am the Way, the Truth, and the life, no on goes to the Father but through Me, open your eyes and you will see Truth, no more lies of the world, God is the Great I Am, The Alpha and Omega, the Beginning and the End, God is the Creator, not the world, and Jesus is the Redeemer not you , you can do nothing unless it is granted to you

Oct 23rd Isn't it wonderful to see love portrayed in pictures and videos, did you know that there is a love that can be with you always, a love that is ever lasting, and eternal. Jesus loves you this way, once you accept His love He will never leave you or forsake you, ever. He has already proved how deep His love is, He died for you, He gave you a part of Himself that will never leave you, He includes His Father who created the world, with Him you have insured victory, He already knows your flaws and still He cannot help but love you, He sees you from the inside not the outside, His love is forever and includes eternity, if you don't know Him find Him, Jesus love is guaranteed, certain, assured, fail safe, and forever

Oct 24th You are chosen as an individual by God to find His Son Jesus, the Messiah, our Savior, our Lord our Redeemer, you don't just walk around the corner and bump into our Wonderful, Gracious Lord, His Father, our Creator draws you to Him, you are loved so much that God sought you out and planted the first seed of remembrance of the life before sin, before satan, before evil, through Grace we return to this relationship with the Trinity, and it is all because of the actions of our Father in Heaven, and His Son Jesus the Messiah, and love is why they are looking for you to open the door

Oct 25th How long do you have to decide for Jesus The Messiah, the rest of the life you have before your physical death, how long do you have to mourn not making that decision, the rest of your spiritual life, the Bible says that in the end every knee shall bow, and every tongue confess that Jesus Christ is Lord, do not take part in the second death, the spiritual death that comes after judgement by our Creator, our Father, Abba. Accept the payment that only Jesus, the only begotten Son of God, could pay, His death on the cross was not in vain, your second death will be, accept Jesus now

Oct 26th The Father and the Son have been together from the beginning; thus, the Holy Spirit has been, all took part in creation, all knew you before the womb, all know you, and all fight for you, and love you. As you accept Jesus, you are accepting all, they are always together, Jesus said if I Am with you who can be against you, this is Truth, believe in Him and believe in Him who sent Him, you were saved by Jesus in the flesh so that flesh can put on immortality again, you have indeed become a new being in Christ Jesus, you can once again commune with Abba Father, Jesus paid that price in the flesh, Jesus chose the pain of the flesh and overcame sin , not for Him, but for you, do you love Jesus, do you love the God, do you love His Spirit who lives in your temple of flesh, they love you

Oct 27th You were created by God, you were deceived by satan, you were rescued by Jesus the Messiah, Jesus was asked by the our Heavenly Father to redeem us, to pay a price, to set us captives free, Jesus has done all His Father asked and more, you have a Way through Jesus, you have a Savior through Jesus, you have a decision about Jesus, after 70 years in Babylon many jews lost their true identity, after the world many of Gods created lost their identity, find out your real identity, find and accept Jesus

Christ and search no more, He has all the answers, He has written down all the answers for you, He will assist you through His Spirit, you will never walk alone again, open your Heart and find out who you really are

Oct 28th Start with Jesus on your mind, not just on your mind, pray, pray for His influence, pray for His guidance, don't let your prayer life become a meaningless habit, pray to Him with purpose every day, tell Him of your needs and the needs of your heart, don't open up a prayer without addressing the Father, our Creator and His Son Jesus, the Messiah, then you can let Them address your Heart while remembrance of your needs will return to your forethoughts instead of your after thoughts, then your heart will tell of needs repressed, our Father knows these needs, Jesus knows these needs, open up to the Trinity, nothing is to small or to large for Them, never say to your self this does not rank Their time, They love you and They care about you, put all your Trust in our Risen Lord and Savior

Oct 29th Everything God created is good, man was good before satan introduces deception in the garden, man was good before sin was introduced in the garden, creation is good, man corrupts it and makes it evil, what ever mans imagination comes up with he does, and satan continues to manipulate man, what do we do to combat this immorality, we can do nothing, however, everything is possible with Jesus, Jesus is the answer to corruption, Jesus is the answer to satan and his deception, Jesus is the answer to your return to God, Jesus will fill you with His Spirit, a Spirit that can not be deceived, a Holy Spirit, you cannot defeat satan alone and with Jesus you will never be alone again, He said He is the Way, the Truth, and the Life, believe this in your heart and be saved

Oct 30th When Gods children come together , why is there sometime discourse, because we have taken our eyes of Jesus, really there is nothing we can do to add to the things that Jesus, the Christ, has already done, Jesus said on the cross it is finished, and it is, look at your heart, don't look outwardly at the world, the world will try to convince you that there is something more you can do, remember you are the saved, not the Savior. The world says to you, yea but, our Lord Jesus Christ says I have already labored and finished it all, when Jesus says all that is what He means, don't let the world tell you that this is not so, Jesus is all Truth, the world will lie, why, because the devil is the fathers of lies, turn to the Truth, turn to Jesus

Oct 31st Listen to the voice of God, listen to the voice of Jesus, listen to the Holy Spirit, you can hear them in your heart, they have already prepared a Way. The Way is secured by our very Creator, the Creator of everything, no physical or spiritual being can prevent your salvation once you have accepted the Way which is another name for Jesus, the only begotten Son of God, His other names are Truth and Life, secure your future, your eternal future through Jesus, you can stop being deceived by man and principalities, stop believing in lies and accept the Truth, and yes it will set you free, free to commune with the Trinity, free to commune with the Truth, free to commune with God, the only God, there are no others, just one

Nov 1st Let me explain this 100% God and this 100% man, His name is Jesus, His origin is in Heaven, He is the only begotten Son of our Creator, our Father and His, who art in Heaven, God asked His Son Jesus to put on the frailty of man to save man from death and eternal separation from the Trinity, Jesus said Father your will be done, so through the Holy Spirit a virgin named mary became pregnant with Jesus and bore the world a Savior, a Savior who paid a price for our sins, a price that we could never pay our self, after all the humiliation and scourging's, Jesus was crucified, cursed and hung on a tree, He died and went to hell, while there He conquered death, He was resurrected by God on the third day and returned to this world for forty days, affirming that He had risen, after forty days He returned to the Fathers Right Hand, and intercedes for man even to this day, HE is the Son of God, He is our Lord and Savior, He will return one day, what a glorious day it will be

Nov 2nd Jesus gave up everything to insure you have the opportunity to have everything, He gave up His life so you could have life, this world is temporary but it is so difficult to give up the temporary for eternity, so many say I will call on Jesus tomorrow, today I have a party to go to with my friends, all the while forgetting the Friend you have in

God Made You

Jesus, the only Friend that will never forsake you or leave you, I pray that tomorrow does come and another chance is given, but remember Jesus was crucified on the cross once and before dying said it is finished, so I pray that tomorrow does come for those that need time with their friends, but what if tomorrow never comes

Nov 3rd Which of your senses tell you there is a God, which tell you there is His Son Jesus our Messiah, all of our senses reveal the glory of the Trinity, can you see, all you see was created by the Trinity, can you feel, all you touch was created by the Trinity, can you smell the fragrance of life, also created by God, do you taste all the wonderful foods provided and created by God, do you hear the birds in the morning, also a creation of Jesus, the Father, the Son, and the Holy Spirit worked in perfect harmony to create all this, and to create you, let me tell you of another sense, that is your heart not your head, your heart it testifies of the Trinity, it fully reveals all of creation and the Creators, not a heart of stone but a heart of flesh, accept Jesus Christ and your heart will be transformed

Nov 4th Do you have a Savior, if you don't there is something missing, without Jesus Christ your life is distorted and deception is right in front of your eyes, you cant feel it or see it, as long as you stay deceived to its reality and true nature, you will never know it exist, yes there are for we wrestle not against flesh and blood, but against **principalities**, against **powers**, against the rulers of the darkness of this world, against spiritual wickedness in heavenly places. you need a Savior who can actually help you defeat satan, that Savior is Jesus Christ, that Savior has already defeated him and will give you a piece of Himself in the form of the Holy Spirit to assist you and open your eyes to the deception of the world, Jesus has your best interest in His heart, the world has no interest in you at all

Nov 5th Would God have asked His only begotten Son to go to the cross for one, He said He would not destroy Sodom and Gomorrah if there were forty, and then again if there was less, and then again if there was less. Gods love is so deep that He would go to the cross for one, you can not find that love in the world, a love that ask nothing in return, a love that would even go to the cross for an enemy, and yes that is exactly what we were before His Son Jesus Christ died on the cross, He didn't die for believers , He died for non-believers, Jesus died for you and me, He died so once again we return to our beginning with God, so we could know our Heavenly Father, Abba, God, our Creator, and the Creator of everything seen and unseen

Nov 6th When your hand slips away from a spouse, another immediately replaces it, when your hand slips away from a loved one ,another immediately replaces it, when you know Jesus, you will know He is always with you, and yes sometimes you only see one set of footprints, and yes they are His, some people say I don't know how I got through this alone, you were not alone, Jesus said He would never leave you or forsake you, unlike the father of lies, there is no lie in Him, He is all Truth, He said I am the Way, the Truth, and the Life, Jesus Christ holds these titles, they were given to Him by our Father who is in Heaven, our Creator, and our God, Jesus Christ did His Fathers will not His own and our Creator testified of what He did for you and I

Nov 7th How could God, God didn't, man did, this is all brought on by mans desire, not Gods. Actually, this is an absence of God, this is an absence of Jesus Christ, this is an absence or the Holy Spirit, when man chooses to live as part of the world his imagination is the limit as to what he may do, he has no moral compass, he has only the father of lies, a deceiver who has nothing but hate. It is easy to say seek God, and people will say, that is what a Christians always says after persecution, those that say that do not know God, they do not know Jesus, they do not know the Holy Spirit, not all are drawn to Gods only begotten Son, if you are seek out Jesus Christ, it is not hard, open the door

Nov 9th So you think you can do it all, only to find you can do nothing without help, Jesus said you can do nothing, that nothing is possible without Him, you cannot accomplish a complete life, a complete fulfillment, anything lasting without the approval of our sovereign God, and you cannot really commune with our Father who is in Heaven without His Son, Jesus said no one goes to the Father except through Me, and it is all Truth, no lie comes from the Throne of God, all lies come from the father of lies, even little white lies, let your influence come from the Heavenly Trinity, Father, Son, and Holy Ghost, not the influence of a liar and deceiver, the devil who wants you to be a failure, seek the Grace of Jesus and your heart will be filled with His love and Grace

Nov 10th Look into your heart, what do you see, how would you answer this question, what would I do if, the if could be anything, and your answer may be right or wrong, you have no guidance if it is only you answering the question, it depends if you have a heart of stone or a heart of flesh, God said I will give you a heart of flesh, that heart of flesh comes through His Son Jesus Christ, Jesus said He will never leave you or forsake you, with Jesus you don't have to answer an if question alone, He is with you always His Holy Spirit lives with in you, you are not alone, if you rely on Him your answer will be correct no matter if, let Him be your saving grace, and faith will grow

Nov 11th Jesus said many will come in my name, or even claiming to be Him, He said don't believe them, He explains in the word of God that everyone will see His return, there will be no deception, one of the gifts of the Holy Spirit is that of discernment, don't just accept things as truth, evil is done in the darkness, perception is blinded by hiding truths, Jesus is the Light of the world, nothing He has done or will do is hidden, everything He has done has been done in the Light if someone or something is hiding truths, they are in fact hiding a lie, Jesus hid nothing and told all Truth, not knowing Jesus, the Truth, is opening yourself up to powers seen and unseen, don't be deceived, accept Jesus as your Lord and Savior

Nov 12th This is what we need to understand, and God did not create us this way, we are inherently evil. When God created us in His Image we where exactly that, but after the fall in the Garden of Eden, after Sin, we lost that image, we took on the image of the fallen one, lucifer sinned against God and so did we, we were both created by God, the difference, satan is a fallen angel, we are a fallen man, the devil has no redemptive qualities in him, man does, thankfully God had a plan for our redemption, His only begotten Son Jesus Christ, through Him we can once again start the process of renewal, once again we can become what we were in the beginning, the Image of God

Nov 13th Today we celebrate what some men have done and are doing for our country and the people of this country, but lets not overlook who has really done for this country and is still doing for this country, His name is a name above all names, His name is Jesus and His fight doesn't end with one deployment or ten, one war or twenty, His fight is for you and me, Jesus said to pontius pilate My Kingdom is not of this world, if it were my servants would fight for Me, well I am a servant of a risen King, I am a servant of Jesus Christ, veteran if you are a servant of Jesus Christ, our Lord and Savior, proclaim His wonderous name, share of His glory and grace, we are no longer on the front line, Jesus stands on that line alone, but your love for Him is felt, share the Love of Jesus Christ, share the love of our Father who art in Heaven, share the love of His Spirit that lives within us, share His story of a His war to save us

Nov 14th When saul had the witch call samual from the grave, samual said why did you wake me from my sleep, when Jesus called lazurus from the grave, lazurus simply obeyed, samual returned to the grave, lazurus lived again in this world and then returned to the grave, let me tell you of our Lord and Savior Jesus Christ, Jesus went to the grave and from there He conquered death, His Father, our Father, who is in Heaven then resurrected His Son, Jesus Christ, from the grave never to return, Jesus sits at the right hand of our Father in Heaven, Jesus said He would return for those that are His, first for the dead, those asleep in the grave, and then the living to forever be with Him, Jesus will resurrect those that are His, we will have no part of the second judgement, Jesus paid it all for us

Nov 15th How much do you know about Jesus Christ, how much do you want to know? The basic is He died for your sins, the how is a different part of the reality of Jesus, He was tortured ,humiliated, spit upon, slapped, verbally assaulted, hung on a tree, cursed by creation, and died through crucifixion, the why is another reality, because His Father asked Him to do these things for man, man that hated, cursed, tortured, and was His Fathers enemy as well as His, and because God so loved the world He gave up His only begotten Son. You were loved when you were unlovable, you were adored when you were unadorable, you were saved when you could not save yourself, accept this gift of life, accept Jesus Christ, He is the Way, the Truth, and The Life, no one goes to the Father except through Him

Nov 16th I devote my life to my Lord and Savior Jesus Christ, through Him I devote my life to His Father who art in Heaven, my God and Creator, through them I receive the Comforter, the Holy Spirit, to guide me and lead me to eternity, in honoring One, you honor the other two, however without the one, you will not feel, see, or talk with the other two, Jesus Christ is the key, He is the Cornerstone, to seek God, you must find Jesus first, Jesus gave all for His Father, Abba, and He gave all for you, He told His Father who is in Heaven, if this cup could pass, but not my will, your will be done, Gods will is for you to be restored to your original image, and through Gods only begotten Son, that image is Gods image, and you are

Nov 17th Creation changes, the leaves change, the weather changes, the seasons change, what doesn't change is Gods love for you, you may not know God, but he still loves you, you may not know God, but He still sent His only begotten Son Jesus Christ to die for you, God loved you when you were unlovable, God loved you when everything else gave up on you, Gods love for you is never changing, what changes is you, God sent His Son so you could once again know Him, once you know Jesus, Jesus sends His Spirit to Help you change back to the image you were created in, you cannot change on your own, but with Jesus change is possible

Nov 18th Why don't people understand, why don't they believe, because deep down they know they will be accountable, the word of God speaks volumes, when you accept Jesus Christ as Lord and Savior those words speak even more, and add the Holy Spirit, even more, people don't want obedience beyond them self's, but Jesus said His burden is light, and it is He has already finished all the requirements for your return home, how can it be any easier or lighter than that, all this was done out of love not malice, how can it get any easier, and by the way, you are already going to be held accountable, creation itself attest to the existence of one sovereign God, let His Son Jesus Christ redeem you, without Him you are guilty

Nov 19th Our sovereign God gave His creation so many chances to redeem ourselves, man failed at all of them, God has provided one last chance, a chance that man cannot fail at, that chance is redemption through Jesus Christ, the only begotten Son of God. The reason man can't fail is because it is your decision rather to accept Jesus Christ or not, you choose rather to be a part of the New Heaven or spend eternity in a bottomless pit of misery in the absence of your Creator, the only one, true God, He is the Alpha and the Omega, man did not create this God, this God created man, and this God created a Way back through His Son Jesus Christ. So just as in this life where you make decisions, you also make the decision to take part in the second death, or not

Nov 20th Jesus said come into His rest, when you accept Him as your Lord and Savior you receive the Holy Spirit which renews you, both physically and spiritually, there is nothing that Jesus Christ has left out, He came as 100% God and 100% man, He knows the flesh and He knows the spirit, He knows how to revive you, He knows the temptations of the flesh, He knows the temptations that come from the spiritual realm, no other has saved you through His crucifixion, no other Has saved you from the grave, which He also conquered, no other has conquered death, His love for you is beyond comparison, His love for His Father and our Father is beyond comparison, accept Jesus fully and become revived

Nov 21st When you pray to our Father who is in Heaven, go through His Son Jesus Christ, this is the Fathers wish, and the Sons deserved right, sometimes we pray that we bless the Father, bless the Father through Jesus His only begotten Son, pray that you are a good and faithful servant to both of Them, when Jesus came in the flesh to save us from death, what He had to endure, but what He gained was worth it to Him and His Father, what He gained was you, accept the gift of life Jesus provided, do not die a second death, how you will die a second death is not the question, the question is how do I prevent dying a second death, the answer, accept Jesus Christ as your

Lord and Savior, He paid the debt you owe, He freed you to return to your home, Heaven

Nov 22nd Jesus has felt total loss, He felt it on the cross, He felt it when He became sin for you, He felt it when His Father turned away, nothing that you endure, no temptation that you have ever had, no loss that you have felt has not been endured, conquered, or felt by your Lord and Savior Jesus Christ, He came so that He would, He came to pay a price you could not, please don't walk through the valley of death without Jesus, He is the Way because He has already conquered death as well, accept Jesus now, one day that opportunity well come and go also

Nov 23rd What is the most important person, place, or thing in your life, can you truly answer with the name of Jesus, can you answer with a New Heaven, can you look forward to an eternity with Jesus Christ, you can if you have accepted Jesus, the only begotten Son of The Great I Am. Get your priority's straight, if you opened your door and Jesus was waiting would you invite Him in, only if you believe that He is your Risen Savior, don't let Jesus be a stranger to you, even if you don't know Him, He knows you, and He loves you just the way you are now, open your heart to Him and you will be revived

Nov 24th Let Jesus help you to change your heart, let Him help you become less of this world and become more of His world, so many people are in doubt because they have loss touch with their Creator, reunite with God by uniting with His Son, become what you were in the beginning, you were not made in the image of this world, we all were made in the image of God, through the sacrifice of His only begotten Son, it is possible to return to the truth through the Truth, Jesus has many names, to know Him is to know the Father, reunite with your first estate

Nov 25th It is thanksgiving, how many will bless their dinner through Jesus Christ, how many ask for every meal they eat to be blessed through Jesus Christ, everyday is a reason to be thankful, thankful that Jesus was willing to pay a price you could not pay, to be thankful in this that God so loved you He gave up His only begotten Son, He gave Him up as a sacrifice to pay for your sins and mine, He sent Him to this world to be born of a virgin, 100% man to live 33 years, a sinless life, only to take on all sin while being crucified on a cross, to die, and be resurrected and return to the right hand side of His Father, our Creator and God, so make this day all inclusive of our Lord and Savior Jesus Christ

Nov 26th Jesus still loves you, Jesus is still knocking, open the door and let your life transform into what it should be instead of what the world wants it to be, when our eyes where opened to the world in the garden we lost a connection with our Creator, regain that connection through His Son Jesus Christ, sin is why we lost the connection with God, forgiveness of sin through our Lord and Savior Jesus Christ is the reconnecting factor of Gods grace, God loved you even why we were still his enemy, become a child of God again and your faith will grow, you will begin to see His grace shower down on you, and begin to love your God again, the one true God, the only God

Nov 27th What gifts are you looking for this year, let me tell you of a few that are free for the asking, salvation, redemption, love, always to be a forethought not an afterthought, all of these gifts are free for the asking, ask Jesus Christ, He is the one that provides these things, not just these things, everything, before you knew him He was already fulfilling many of these gifts, He has always known you and waits for you to respond to His love every second of everyday, Jesus waits on you, without Him you have no eternal identity, there is life after this world of doubt, doubt no more, accept Jesus Christ, and these gifts and more will revive your life

Nov 28th What if there was no Jesus, what if God never sought us again after we failed Him? man would do what ever his imagination came up with, we wouldn't have any good, all would be evil, and satan would rule, there would not be any good in your heart of stone. Thank God for second chances, thank Jesus His Son for third, fourth, fifth chances, Jesus was asked, how many times do we forgive, His reply, seven times seventy, meaning forever, you are forgiven, accept Jesus's sacrifice, accept the blood He shed for you, Jesus did die on the cross, but He conquered death, He conquered death for you, and now He sits at the right hand of His Father, our Father and God, and He waits for you with out stretched arms and a Holy kiss, accept Jesus as your Lord and Savior

Nov 29th There is a solution to every need you will ever have and that is Jesus Christ, there is an answer to every question you will ever have and that is Jesus Christ, alone you can not do anything because you don't have the support system to accomplish them, Jesus Christ endured both physical and mental torture to develop that support system, a system for everyone, that support system is a renewed relationship with our Father who art in Heaven, our Creator, the only one True God, this system insures eternity in the presence of The Father and the Son and the Holy Spirit, in the end they will be our total and only support

Nov 30th Everyone speaks with total confidence on any religion they are part of, and people say it is their right, when people speak of a relationship with a God, the only true God, they are persecuted, that relationship is called Christianity, it is not controlled by man, it is not an invention of man, it did not come from the imagination of man. It started when our Creator sent His only begotten Son to pay a price no man could ever pay, which He did with His blood, Jesus provided the Way back to a relationship with our Heavenly Father, forgiveness came through the actions of Jesus and it is yours for free, embrace your Lord and Savior and start a relationship not a religion

God Made You

Dec 1st Are we so smart that we can support ourselves, are we so technologically advanced that we don't need a Savior, they say that space is the last frontier, I will tell you they are wrong, the last frontier is life after this world, the last frontier is knowing or not knowing our Heavenly Father, the last frontier is knowing or not knowing His only begotten Son Jesus Christ, you see there is an eternity and that eternity will be spent in the presence of our Savior or in the absence of our Savior, all will have known Him but there will be a time when there is not another chance, every knee will bow and every tongue confess that Jesus Christ is Lord, there will be a final judgement for those that do not accept Jesus as Lord

Dec 2nd When Jesus came to die for our sins did He know if it would do any good, would He save even one, after all we were enemies of His Father and Himself, God had given us the freedom to choose, nobody knew Him, and in the end we turned against Him and sent Him to a cross instead of a murderer , yet He did the Fathers will, I hope today you are one of the believers, I hope today you have accepted Jesus Christ as your Lord and Savior, even while hanging on a tree Jesus asked Father forgive them, they know not what they do, accept Jesus He has proven His love, the world has proven nothing

Dec 3rd What do you and I have to do with the world, having nothing to do with the world why does the world choose to attack my Lord and Savior Jesus Christ always and only His followers Christians the reason is this, the world did not create Him, He created the world, more specifically why does man attack their creator, in the beginning man was perfect, the father of lies brought imperfection into perfection and continues to this day, deception comes from him, Jesus will open your eyes to reality, He will show you who you are made to be, don't continue believing the lies that the world constantly reminds you of, return to perfection, return to your perfection, that perfection comes through Jesus Christ, the only begotten Son of our Father Abba

Dec 4th Wake up in celebration, if you belong to Jesus Christ every morning is a blessing, wake up and praise His Holy name, He alone is worthy, through Him you honor His Father, our Creator, our God, Jesus did the will of His Father and in doing sent a blessing that will last you into eternity, know Jesus as Lord and become a member again of His Holy Family, once again through Jesus we can commune with our God, the only God that has ever existed, through Him we are once again apart of His heavenly Father, and yes Jesus is the reason for the celebration of His earthly birth

Dec 5th Christian, why are we letting the devil win, why is the name of Jesus, the only begotten Son of God, so passé, proclaim the name of Jesus, He proclaims your name to our Father every day, don't let an opportunity to tell the lost how they can be found, how Jesus provided an escape, how He paid a price for your redemption, a price you or I could never pay, don't let the lies of satan win over the truths of Jesus, you wouldn't let people tell lies about your family, don't let people tell lies about your Lord and Savior Jesus Christ, quit sitting on the fence, don't be lukewarm. Proclaim the name of Jesus, how many likes can Jesus get

Dec 6th As far as I know there is only one church body, as far as I know there is only one Holy bible, as far as I know there is only one Head to church body and that is Jesus Christ, so were does all this difference come from, lets start with where it didn't come from, it did not come from Jesus Christ He is all Truth, it didn't come from the written word of our Father who is in Heaven, it tells all Truth, it came from the body, it came from man, reading the front cover of our Lords word does not make an expert of the rest of His words, reading all of His words does not make an expert, Jesus Christ said you can do nothing without Him, through Him you are given a Teacher in the person of the Holy Spirit, this is where understanding and discernment come from, through the Trinity, The Father, The Son, and the Holy Spirit, not from the world but from Heaven, The very Throne of God

Dec 7th There is someone writing about Jesus, you look at it as you casually go by it, do you give a second thought of who He is, of what He did, of the pain He endured for you, it is easy to continue down a road that has no requirements, that road does have a requirement and it is death, it is eternity alone, but I never knew, you knew, the problem you never became new through Jesus Christ, so you decided to stay in the dead body you live in, not a temple for the Holy Spirit, just a home for a decaying soul, seek Jesus out and find the Godhead, find Jesus and renew yourself, making yourself presentable for your Creator once again, God will not look upon sin and through Jesus Christ blood your sins are washed away

Dec 8th Man will leave you, man will forsake you, Jesus Christ said I will never leave you or forsake you, Jesus Christ is all Truth, who should you follow? makes perfect sense to me, don't accept temporary, don't accept now with out eternity, Jesus is the Way, the Truth, and the Life and He will lead you to our Father, our Creator, our Beginning and End, nothing is temporary in our Gods name, there is only one and He is the Father of Jesus and the Father of all creation, Jesus is Love, God is Love, and the Holy Spirit is Love, they will not leave you or forsake you, ever.

Dec 9th Our Father who are in Heaven, put your peace on those that need it find those that don't know you, just give them a little piece of Heaven, oh you have, you have in your Son Jesus Christ, help us to draw strength from Him, you have, you have in your Spirit, you7 have provided peace, I pray that all will learn to find this peace, oh, they can Jesus said He is knocking, He is knocking at your personal door, He is available to us as an individual, His love helps us to endure the impossible, impossible for us, entirely possible for Jesus, rely on Jesus and receive the strength of the Father, Son, and Holy Spirit

God Made You

Dec 10th Is it to hard to understand that you have a Savior that requires nothing of you but belief in Him, Jesus Has done everything for you, including those things which you could never do yourself, He even died for you, and yes He was tormented for you, a lot of the times by you, He prayed Father forgive them, they know not what they do, the knowledge of Jesus Christ does not insure life, the knowledge and acceptance of Jesus Christ does, it is a free gift, no works are required of you, you can do none that will add anything to His accomplishments, He fulfilled for your Salvation, Jesus said it is finished and when He said it He was all alone, He did this for your salvation not His, accept Him as your Lord

Dec 11th Jesus needs no reminders, He is thinking of you, He will be thinking of you from now until eternity, why or why you did not choose Him and what He freed you from, why you chose a dying world over salvation through Him, of course He already knows the answer because in the end, rather you chose Him or not, you will confess, every knee will bow and every tongue confess that Jesus, our risen Savior, is Lord, in the end everyone will know the Truth, the question is did you let Truth set you free, Jesus is the Way, the Truth, and the Life, no one goes to the Father but through the Son

Dec 12th Is it really all about Jesus Christ, yes it is, Jesus died for our sins, not His, He sacrificed Himself so we would not have to endure the punishment we rightly deserve, a life without Jesus is a life that has no gauges of morality, as God said in His Holy word, what ever our imaginations leads us to do we would do, our minds would be pure evil because there would be no conduit back to our Heavenly Father, you would die twice and in the end you would be in a bottomless pit of misery, forever absent from a God that you would only met once, and that would be judgement day, Jesus said seek and you will find, so seek out Jesus and begin your resurrection back to an eternity with our Trinity

Dec 13th Look around you and you will know that the words of the bible are God spoken, the world is in spiritual decay, they are in fact doing what ever their imagination comes up with, man cannot change creation so they change the words that describe creation, words like gender neutral, and same sex marriage, and perverting the very words of God in our classrooms, they are trying to erase the very existence of our Lord and Savior Jesus Christ, they do not know Him but still He offends them, Christian stand up and be recognized, be counted as one that is counted as belonging to the only God in existence and His Son, our Lord and Savior, Jesus Christ, don't be ashamed of your decision to become a new person in Christ, let them be ashamed of not becoming a new person in Christ

Dec 14th Don't ignore Jesus when He calls, don't say just one more time around the block, going out never changes, your life with Jesus Christ will change you daily and it will change you for the better, you will truly begin to love your neighbor as yourself, life will become happier and you wont just look forward to the weekend, you will look forward to everyday, with the Holy Spirit guidance you will begin to see and experience life with a new outlook, a better outlook, a spiritual outlook instead of a carnal outlook, when Jesus knocks open the door and invite Him in to your life

Dec 15th It seems all interest is in christmas and not the reason for Christmas, is everything that commercial that our Lord and Savior can not get recognition, the reason for this is a celebration, a celebration of not only who Jesus Christ is but what He did, Honor Jesus for doing something for us we could not do ourselves, Honor Him for who He is, the only begotten Son of God, born of a virgin in Bethlehem, living a life as a Witness and Servant, and dying for something we did, not Him, on a cross, conquering death, and being resurrected to the right hand of the Throne of God, His Father and our Father and Creator, paving a path for us back to Glory

Dec 16th Is it because you don't see Him or is it you don't want to see Him because once you see Him you will also see yourself, our Lord and Savior doesn't care what you look like, He wants you just the way you are, you cannot perfect your flaws, but He can and wants to, our King and Saviors name is Jesus, the only begotten Son of God and God has given Him the power to save, yes even you

Dec 17th It is hard, look toward your Savior, look toward your Lord, Jesus called Lazarus out, Jesus was standing for

Steven as He was martyred, Jesus is King of Kings, Lord of Lords, Jesus said He would never leave us or forsake us, a loved ones hand may slip from yours only to slip into Jesus's out stretched hand, only for a moment, a blink of an eye, will absence be felt, He conquered death, if you belong to Jesus you to will conquer it all while walking with our Savior, there will be a reunion, there will be rejoicing once again, assurance in Jesus is assurance for eternity

Dec 18th I'm glad that Jesus is no longer 100% man and 100% God, He has been transformed, He does not give up, He does not quit, He sees no reason to stop, He is fully committed to you 100 % of the time, Jesus will never forget about you, He said and it bares repeating, He will never leave you or forsake you, Jesus Christ loves you, the only begotten Son of God adores you, and He died to save you, but till death do us part does not apply here, He said I am going to prepare a place for you and if I am preparing a place for you I will come back for you, Jesus is all Truth, He will return

Dec 19th No time in your busy life to even focus on Jesus for a second, that second can change your life, that second will determine your destiny, that second tells the Creator of this and everything seen and unseen that you accept what His only begotten Son paid for you, it is a free gift from Heaven, it is not wrapped or hidden in a pretty bag, what is given to you is visible, open your heart and that will open your eyes, Jesus will give you this gift of life if you sitting in a ditch with a bottle in your hand or at a party in a penthouse high above the street, He accepts you as you are, you don't need to dress up or dress down, all you need to do is accept Him

Dec 20th Do you think you have it all figured out, be careful, in the twinkling of an eye the world can change, man is capable of doing what ever their mind imagines, man has no surety about him, you will never find stability in man, where can you go to find assurance, open your heart to Jesus, He is all Truth and what ever He promises soon will be reality, what ever He says is Truth, and His love is real, what Jesus says He does, and what He does will last an eternity, He is the Sacrifice for your sins, He is the only begotten, He conquered death for you and me, and He offers Salvation, so seek out your Lord and Savior and you will be redeemed

Dec 21st How long will Jesus wait for a response to His invitation of Life, He waits sometime a lifetime and receives not even a glance, but still He gives everyone the opportunity to accept Him for who He is , the Lord and Savior of all, appointed to this position by a loving Father, the only True God, a Creator not a creation, with all this Holy Royalty Jesus still waits for a response to His cry to save you, His love for you is the only reason He waits, man the created would have given up long ago, but Jesus King of Kings, Lord of Lords, still waits on you, open your heart and let Him revive you

Dec 22nd Open your eyes without Jesus and see nothing, open your eyes with Jesus and see everything, with The Holy Spirit you don't have to ask why, why do bad things happen, because bad people do them, why is there evil, because evil people exist, they have no guidance nor do they think they need it, Gods word is a direction, it is a guide, without Jesus you will not understand his Fathers words, without Jesus no teacher is given, without the Holy Spirit we would remain lost and satan would have his victory, to accomplish anything you need Jesus, He is the Cornerstone, accept Him and receive life

Dec 23rd What are the benefits of accepting Jesus Christ, you are saved from a world that has no love for you or care about you, you are no longer just a statistic, you are saved from an eternity of sorrow and pain in a bottomless pit designed for fallen angels, and after the garden fallen men, you are grafted back into the tree of Life, all offences against our God are forgiven never to be seen again, you will spend eternity in Heaven where there is no pain and no tears, you no longer look for creation to provide now the Creator provides, God who made everything seen or not seen, bottom line there are no benefits to not accepting Jesus Christ as your Lord and Savior

Dec 24th Why does Jesus always come back, He doesn't, He never left you, He is still watching and waiting for you to stop and turn His way, He is all love, so He waits on you, a King waits on you, a King of Kings waits on you,

God Made You

Jesus Christ wants you to live the way you were created to live, why is it so important to Him to wait, to wait on you, because your alternative is death, Jesus conquered death and through Him you can also conquer death, you are why He waits

Dec 25th I'm devoted to my Heavenly King, King of Kings, Lord of Lords, His name is Jesus, Christ, Messiah, The Way, The Truth, The Life, He came from Heaven to Earth and chose the life of a man, He chose to do His Fathers will. He chose to live a sin free life only to become sin on the cross, He chose to sacrifice His Life so we can spare our life, freely given to you, you need only to accept this gift, a gift that originated in Heaven, a gift that frees you from a second death, a spiritual death, open your hearts to Jesus just the way you are, He knows you as you are and still gives this gift of life, no works you do will add or subtract anything, this gift in Jesus Christ is complete and it will complete you, repent and accept Jesus

Dec 26th I cannot tell you the exact hour or day my Savior was born, I can tell you for certainty that my Savior was born, I can tell you for certainty that my Savior was born to a woman named Mary, I can tell you for certainty that a man never touched Mary, I can tell you my Savior was born to live and die for me and you, I can tell you for certain that my Savior was tempted more than I will ever be and yet did not sin, I can tell you for certainty that my Savior took on my sins and paid for my transgressions and yours and died on a cross, I can tell you for certain that

God Made You

Jesus the only begotten Son of our Father who is in Heaven sacrificed Himself so once again I can reunite with our Creator and God, I can tell you that all this is true because the word of God tells me so and that there is not a lie in Him, therefore there is not a lie in His word, believe and you will be set free

Dec 27th If we put the energy into our own salvation that we do in tracking santa claus we all would be saved, sadly the majority of the world does not, some don't know Jesus Christ, some don't care to know Him, I'll tell you there is only one way to continue life and life in abundance and that is to accept Jesus as your personal Savior and Lord, it is simple say yes to Jesus, say yes to the free gift of salvation He gave you, there is no stronger love than to die for a friend, Jesus died for us, He was the final sacrifice, He is the Beginning and the End

Dec 28th Well a new year will be starting soon, many people will make resolutions, many of which will fail, most resolutions fail because there is no support system, resolve to accept Jesus Christ as your Savior and Lord and you are given a support system that will never leave you, you have no phone number to call for support, you don't have to drive anywhere for support, your support is where you are always, your support has a name, it is the Holy Spirit, He will teach you, He will show you, He will support you always, Jesus said He would not leave you or forsake you, Jesus will stay with you from now until eternity, Jesus will be with you always

Dec 29th What can we do to make this year a better year, repent and be saved, hear the Heaven rejoice, rejoice over you, yes rejoice over you, Jesus Christ already knows you inside and out, all your darkest secrets, and He still loves you and wants you just the way you are, He will perform the miracle in your life, He will transform you, He will give you a knew mind and a new body, He will make you perfect, He will give you hope, He will give you love that you have not known, He will never leave you or forsake you, with Jesus you cannot lose, make this a year you will never forget, make this a year of rejoicing, make this the year you gave your life to Jesus

Dec 30th Do you have to go at it alone, cant get anyone to support you, Jesus accomplished all He did by Himself, one thing that separates what He did from what you may be attempting, it wasn't His plan, it was His Fathers will, and Jesus said not My will but Your will be done, Jesus served His Father and He served you and me, Jesus came to serve, and He did all the way to death and beyond, His life on earth was for you, He paid a price you or me could never pay, it wasn't His debt, it was our debt, He gave us a gift of life, life abundant and forever, He holds His Holy hand out to you, if you have already accepted His gift you can relate because you are a relative of Jesus Christ, if you have not accepted this free gift from God do it and realize the Truth that will set you free

Dec 31st It is very basic today, Jesus died for you not Himself, Jesus endured hardship and torture for you not

Himself, Jesus took on your sin not His own, Jesus conquered death for you not Himself, Jesus became the final sacrifice for you not Himself, He did these things knowing that all of us where His enemies, Jesus is giving you a chance to make your life perfect through no actions of your own, a free gift waiting for you to accept and open, many will see this gift of salvation and never open it, many will even touch this gift only to be distracted and deceived by a false gift, accept Jesus and become what you where always meant to be

Jan 1st If you will listen you will here the Holy Spirit, if you look you will see Jesus's guidance, if you touch you will know God is present, if you do not search you will not find, He said search His words, Jesus said that He will not leave you or forsake you, His words are true, so who is doing the leaving and the forsaking, you are, you can sense when you are not in the presence of the Holy Trinity and you make a choice to continue on a path of destruction or return to the grace which Jesus provides, return to His graces, fast And pray, seek Him and you will find Jesus, open the door and let Him in

Jan 2ndSome people say it is a good read, they have no belief, some people say it is fiction, they have no faith, the only belief they have is of this world so they are part of this world and believe lies from the father of lies, the words of our Creator, the words of our Lord and Savior Jesus Christ are all true, a lie cannot exist in them, they are all Truth, acceptance of the Truth leads to Salvation through Jesus, Salvation through Jesus leads to Grace from our Father who is in Heaven, this Grace leads to a relationship with all three to include the Holy Spirit who dwells in you, the Holy Spirit teaches more and more Truth through the words of God, our Holy Bible, accept, read, and believe, belief leads to an eternal life with God, Jesus, and the Holy Spirit, unbelief leads to a second death and a bottomless pit of despair

Jan 3rd There is nothing that happens that is not ordained by our Creator, our God, God does not just let events just happen, everything in life is a call to return to Him and His Glory, in order to accept God you must accept His Son Jesus, Jesus said no one goes to the Father accept through me, why Has God given His Son this power, Jesus did His Fathers will onto death, He took on all the sins of the world, past, present, and future, and was sacrificed on a cross, not because of anything He did, He died for everything we did, He too k sin to the grave with Him, there is no other way, Jesus said He is the Way, there is no other Truth, there is no other Life, accept Jesus Christ as your Lord and Savior

Jan 4th It is a new year, that is mans word for another year, God said there is nothing new under the sun, what was will be again, there is only one way to receive something new, accept Jesus Christ as your Lord, accept Jesus Christ as your Savior, when you do this you will receive something new, a new heart, one that is no longer made of stone but a heart of flesh, a new body, not one that will perish with this earth but one that will be transformed into glory with Jesus, new thoughts, thoughts that come from the word of God, thoughts that are made clear through the Holy Spirit, if you want new accept the Son of God into your life

Jan 5th God has blessed you with another day, there is still time, we can still tell the seasons, there is still time, this may be your last day, there is still time, there is still time to accept Jesus Christ as your Lord and Savior, He wants you just the way you are, if repentance is true and from your heart you can be saved just the way you are, why and how, Jesus, He paid the price, with Him all is forgiven and forgotten forever, Jesus is the answer, He has always been the answer from the Garden of Eden to now and beyond, find Jesus, find Life

Jan 6th There is a song that says I did it my way, that is one of the problems, you did it your way and failed, you will always fail if you do it your way, Jesus Christ said I am the Way, so who is telling the truth, Jesus my Savior said I am the Truth, so is it your truth or The Son of God's Truth that will set you free, there is no way possible for anyone toad to the price that Jesus paid for you on a cross in calvary, if there was our Creator, our God, our Father who art in Heaven would not have had to sacrifice His only Begotten Son, as a matter of fact He started with man and man could not follow one of His laws, Jesus is the Way, the Truth, and the Life, no one goes to the Father without first going to the Son, accept Jesus as your Lord and Savior and become what you were meant to be

Jan 7th Some don't know of our Lord and Savior, some don't want to know Him, why, knowing Him will interfere with their life style, to know Him is to love Him, to love Him is to follow Him, Jesus Christ does not force Himself upon you, you have free will, God does not force Himself upon you, you have free will, They will not make the choice for you, the decision is yours, eternity is your decision, Jesus said ask and you will receive, many will die because they refused to ask, His word is not hidden, His creation can not be hidden, you will make the decision to follow Him or not, one day it will be to late, seek Jesus today

Jan 8th What is the most important item to talk about today, your salvation is, a lot of people think that their good works and deeds will get them to the new Heaven, Jesus Christ said no one is good but the Father, so that rules out goodness, as Jesus Christ was about to give up His last earthly breath while being crucified for you and me He said it is finished, that pretty much takes away works. As a matter of fact, which is Truth, the words of God says that anyone, angel or man, that adds to or takes away, to or from His word, will be accursed, the only way to reach Heavenly Paradise is to commit to Jesus the only begotten Son of God our Father, Jesus said no one goes to the Father except through Him, and that is Truth, if you don't know Jesus seek Him out

God Made You

Jan 9th Lord I ask that you walk with us through life, Jesus said where two or more are gathered I am also with them, Jesus said He would not forsake you or leave you, in acceptance of Jesus Christ a portion of Himself abides in the temple, or abides in you in the form of the Holy Spirit, He is always with you, where two or more are gathered the grace of God is with you, His only begotten Son and His Spirit, you are not alone anywhere in the world and in any situation you find yourself in, Jesus Christ said if I am for you who can be against you, Jesus Christ is Truth, belief in Him will sustain you forever, even to the end, when all is in Christ hand and He returns all to His Father our God a new Heaven and a New earth will be ours in Glory with the Trinity

Jan 10th If we follow Jesus's examples we can only benefit, Jesus never did anything half way, He committed till completion even unto death, He didn't just take on half our sins, He took on all our sins, it didn't matter how minute they were they had the same importance as all the rest, to His Father and our Father who is in Heaven a sin was a sin, they are not categorized, they are all the same, He does not categorize us, to Him we are all the same ,sinners, the difference is those that have accepted Him as King, Lord and Savior, those that know Him to be the only begotten Son of God, those that took the free gift of forgiveness He provided when He was crucified, conquered death, and was resurrected back to life to forever sit at the right hand side of the throne of God, He is deserving to be called King of Kings, lord of Lords and Savior

Jan 11th What Jesus Christ has done for you and me is not mentioned by the religions of this world, what He did and accomplished at Calvary is not documented in any of this worlds religious books, why, because man wrote those religious books with the help of the father of lies, if all those books are a lie where can you find the Truth, in the living word of our Creator, our God, the only God that man didn't imagine into existence, the only True God and there is only one, His words tell us of His only begotten Son, His word tells how His Son came to earth to take on the sins of the world, to the crucifixion of His Son at Golgotha, to His Son's conquering of death, and of His Son's resurrection back to the Throne in Heaven, so read fiction or Truth, accept your Savior or die a second time, the choice is yours, your creator gave you free will, so you choose, creation is proof of the Creator our God, and our God's word is proof of His Son

Jan 12th What is wrong with this world, it is missing something, it has no guidance, it doesn't look for guidance, the world does what ever the imagination of man decides , and these men also have no guidance, the guidance they are missing is the Holy Spirit, some choose to ignore the Spirit of Jesus when they feel that they have overcome the need and fade away just like the seed thrown on rocky soil, they had no commitment to our Lord and Savior Jesus Christ, once you accept the King of

God Made You

Kings Lord of Lords it doesn't become a one sided affair, you may have heard His knock and opened the door, only to turn and shut the next behind you, Jesus is totally committed to you, become totally committed to Him

Jan 13th Jesus was looking down when steven was martyred, He wasn't only looking down, He was standing, ready to bring him through the valley of death, when steven left this world he was joined by the Lord of Lords, King of Kings, and his personal Savior Jesus Christ, yes we are personal to Jesus, He loves us with an undying love, not just collectively but individually, He knows every hair on your head, He loves all of us including those that don't know Him and those that are His enemy, He died for all of us through crucifixion, a slow painful death through torture, if you don't know Jesus , the only begotten Son of God, get to know Him, let Him into your life and your heart, let Him save you from this dying world

Jan 15th What on this earth can you count on 100% of the time, the answer is nothing, the only guarantee you have when you are born is that you will some day die, let me tell you of a guarantee that will always hold true, that guarantee is Jesus Christ, when you accept Him you can count on Him forever, His guarantee's come from the very Throne room of God, they are Truth, they will be, there is no doubt, there is not a maybe, there is not a waiting period, Jesus was before creation, Jesus is always, when there is a new Heaven and a new earth He will be, His guarantee is for eternity, He said ask and you shall receive, no better guarantee exist, accept Jesus as your Savior and reps the benefits of a true Life

Jan 16th I woke up this morning and said good morning Lord, I asked how did you sleep, His reply was I watched over you as you slept, He said I will never forsake you or leave you, once you have accepted Jesus Christ as your Lord and Savior He is with you always, 24 hours a day, seven days a week, you were His main priority as He died on a cross and you are still His main priority, Jesus is committed to you, you will not find this commitment anywhere but with Him, His commitment to you is everlasting, make your commitment to Him everlasting, not just when it is convenient for you, convenience is not commitment, love Jesus as He loves you

Jan 17th Whatever your situation, Jesus Christ still loves you, no matter how sick you are Jesus Christ still loves you, no matter how close to death you are Jesus Christ still loves you, as a matter of fact, as we get closer and closer to death we grow closer and closer to Him, Jesus doesn't draw closer to you because when you accept Jesus as your Lord and Savior He is as close to you that day as He will be the day you die, you may not remember Him when you go on vacation but you sure want Him when you battle death, He has defeated death and through Him you also can defeat death forever, draw closer to Jesus every day, take Him on that vacation, take Him to work, take Him every where you go, He is King of Kings lord of Lords. If He is for you who can be against you

God Made You

Jan 18th If you want a stress free life ever after find Jesus, this life on earth is but a second of eternity, know that you are redeemed by a Redeemer, know that you belong to a King who is above all kings, one of His titles is King of Kings Lord of Lords, Jesus Christ is a conqueror, He has conquered death, He has put satan behind Him, follow a Risen Lord to Eternity don't follow a defeated adversary, don't believe the lies of the father of lies he has been defeated, Jesus is all Truth, He knows His Father, He knows our Father and He paid the price of redemption for you, God did not give His only begotten Son up for Him to be ridiculed or unnoticed, for redemption you must accept Him for who He is, for what He has done, and where He is, He is the only begotten Son of the only God that has ever existed, that Jesus did come to live the same life as you and do it sin free, that He was the only perfect sacrifice to pay for the sins you committed, that He did die, that He did conquer death, and that He was resurrected back to the right Hand side of God who is our Father who is in Heaven, that Jesus is the only Way

Jan 19th He waits, Jesus waits on you, He has already made His decision, He has already paid the price for sin, not His price your price, He has already declared that He is preparing a place for you in Heaven, He has done all these things in anticipation of your decision, in anticipation of your answer, do you accept this free gift of salvation the only begotten Son of God offers you, Jesus Christ has secured your future, do you want it , do you accept Him for who He is, or do you believe the lies of this world, do you believe the lies of the father of lies, satan, where there is no future besides a bottomless pit, the Truth can be seen, a lie never existed

Jan 20th Jesus Christ said He would take you to greener pastures, didn't He provide that when He cleansed you with His own blood, what greener pastures are there other than Heaven itself, He will lie you down beside still waters, you will have no worries there, no tears just grace and love, peace, a peace you have always wanted, a peace that does not exist on this earth, you are perfected, you are transfigured, all can see, all can walk, all are made whole, grace is overflowing, accept the gift of Life Jesus provides, be renewed, refreshed, and born again

Jan 21st The majority of the world does not believe in Jesus Christ or what He did for us on calvary, the majority of the world doesn't believe because they don't know, tell someone today, don't be ashamed of our Risen Lord and Savior, don't feel like it isn't worth it because it does no good, if only one is saved you have added to the Kingdom of God, Christian stand up for the power of Jesus Christ, in prayer when you feel His presence isn't it awesome, He does not hide Himself, the creation of what we see involved all three, The Father, The Son, and The Holy Spirit, they are not Hiding, Their glory and Grace is visible if you open your eyes and your heart, spread the good news

God Made You

Jan 22nd I am glad that Jesus Christ is not a quitter, I am glad He only accepts success, that He stays until He determines it is finished, Jesus said it is finished, what was finished, He had finished paying the price of a sinner, not His sins your sins, through Jesus Christ we do not need to die a second death, when you accept Jesus Christ for who He is and what He has done you are saved, it doesn't matter how you are dressed, what color your skin is, or what sin you come burdened with, He will make you anew, His success becomes your success, you become a joint heir in paradise, you will be made whole, you where perfect in the beginning, you will be perfect in the end

Jan 23rd Christian don't conform to the world, conform to Jesus Christ our Lord, God's word says if we humble ourselves then He will hear us and answer us, the world does not want to hear about there faults because in their hearts of stone they have no faults, they will never see their faults, we can not soften their hearts and give them hearts of flesh, Jesus does have this capacity though, He is King of Kings Lord of Lords, with Him we can accomplish anything, without Him we can accomplish nothing, when you go into this world pray and take the Armor of God with you Jesus, The Holy Spirit, and Our Father who is in Heaven, don't go with out them or you will be blamed for the worlds faults, take them with you and the world will see their faults, prayer is the first thing to put on each morning then the ensembles of the Armor of God can follow, pray Christian

God Made You

Jan 24th Remember one thing you can not serve two masters, in the case of this world one master is full of deceptions and lies, you do not see these lies because you don't know the truth, Jesus said there is no truth in them, if you want to know the truth get to know the Truth, Jesus Christ said I am the Way the Truth and the Life, so if you want to know the Truth get to know the Truth who is Jesus the only begotten Son of God, the Truth will set you free, your eyes will be opened and your heart will be made flesh, there is no reality in this world, to truly see you must accept Jesus as your Lord and Savior, He has paid the price, He will set you free, with Jesus as your King your eyes will be opened to the Truth

Jan 25th On the cross Jesus said it is finished, did He lie, the words of God says that any man or angel that adds or subtracts from His words will be accursed, who is john smith, who is the angel he met in the forest, what are the golden tablets he was given, satan will disguise himself as an angel of light, the devil will accuse you at the throne of God, satan will mimic God as he sees the opportunity, who is muhammad that he rewrites the word of God, deception and trickery will be employed by satan when he sees no opposition, for those that don't know his opposition is Jesus Christ and satan knows he has already been defeated, Jesus Christ is all Truth, there is no lie in Him, the only sin He ever had was yours, look into the word of God, listen to the word of God, Jesus provides all you need to enter the grace of God, please accept Him while we have time, death is a certainty , and the return of Jesus Christ is certain, don't wait the invitation is given to all

Jan 26th Jesus doesn't want to hear from you when you are in need, He wants to hear from you always, in good times and bad, He wants you as you are, in the morning, in the evening, all day long, Jesus Christ is interested in you always, His love for you is everlasting, does it hurt you when people forget about you, well it hurts Him to, does it hurt you when you are left out, it hurts Him to, Jesus knows all of these feelings first hand, He was hated, He was rejected, He was emotionally drained, Jesus lived through all these things to set you free, seek His face always because He will always be there for you, His love does not and will not die for you, He will wait forever to see your smile, accept Him as Lord and Savior, He will change your life forever

Jan 27th Man had nothing to do with creation other than being created, if you study the Word of God you will see that the Father, Son, and Holy Spirit were the Creators, some items were spoken into existence, man was made from dust. A part of the created, if something can be spoke into existence why cant it be spoken out of existence, because God gave man free will, man is why Jesus came from the Throne of Heaven to live as a man, only living in a way man could not, sin free, He was subjected to mans torture and crucified on a cross to pay a price the created could not, He was an atoning sacrifice not for His sins but mans sins, the Creator became the created to set us free, opening a Way back to Father who art in Heaven, don't deny Jesus Christ praise the King of Kings for what He did, reach out to Him and find comfort that exist no where else, His undying love

Jan 28th Were does your strength lie, in this world it may be in leadership, it may be in physical work, it may be intellectual, all these strengths will come to an end, rely on a strength that will never diminish, a strength that is forever, that strength is in Jesus Christ the only begotten Son of God, He has defeated all His adversaries, He has defeated the world, He has defeated mans opposition to Him, He has defeated death, He has defeated all spiritual opposition, He has defeated the devil, He has not lost, and, He used all His strength for you, and, He uses all His strength for you still, He is Truly King of Kings Lord of Lords, He is your Savior, accept Him today, open the door to your heart and let Him reign

Jan 29th The fact is we are not capable, we never could save ourselves, God has given us so many chances to return to Him on our own, we tried and we failed, we had sank so deep into the depravity of satans lies we don't even know how to begin, there seems to be no hope, there is Hope, there seems to be no way, there is a Way, the Hope and the Way is provided by Jesus Christ , He is the only way, you can find everything you need through Him and in Him, He loves you and wants to provide this to you just the way you are, if you are broke, He will fix you,

He will provide, accept Him, accept Him today, and begin life anew

Jan 30th Jesus Christ is King of Kings, Jesus Christ is Lord of Lords. Jesus Christ is the only begotten Son of God, Jesus Christ is the Way, Jesus Christ is the Truth, Jesus Christ is the Life, Jesus Christ is the last Sacrifice, Jesus Christ is, what are you waiting for, the invitation has been given, everything has been paid for, eternity is free, all you need do is repent and believe, ask for forgiveness, asked to be washed by His atoning blood, Jesu has done everything for you, the table is set, the King waits for you to take your seat, and yes it is up to you, it is your choice, it is your decision, Jesus's hand is open, take it and let your eyes and heart open to reality, Jesus is the only answer, all of this is Truth

Jan 31st Looking for more energy today, pray, looking for some enthusiasm, pray, looking for guidance pray, pray fervently, pray, pray, pray, who are you praying to, our Father who art in Heaven, who's will are you praying to be done, Jesus stated if this cup could pass by Him, but not His will but our Fathers will be done, Jesus said He would not leave us and He would not forsake us, the answer you seek may not be the best answer, the answer you receive from the only true God is the answer you need, if you are a servant of our risen Lord and Savior all your needs will be taken care of, you will be blessed beyond your imagination, when Jesus is your King three are praying for you, the Holy Spirit is praying for you, Jesus is praying for you, and you are praying for you, become an adopted child of God, accept Jesus Christ, complete your prayer life through Him, without Him they are just words

Feb 1st There is room for everyone in the house of the Lord, Jesus said He is going to prepare a room for you, He has opened His Heavenly home to you already, He has given you an invitation and He sealed it with His blood, not wax, not glue, but a piece of Himself, everything He has done for us is endorsed by out Heavenly Father, the only True God, don't say I didn't know, creation attest to the Creator, and the Creator attest to His only begotten Son, read the very words of Gods and light will begin to illuminate the Truth, it will reveal a path back to union with our Father who is in Heaven, a part of the Trinity of Christ, open your eyes to the Truth, open your eyes to Jesus and never be blind again

Feb 2nd Jesus Christ is waiting on you and he'll wait for eternity it's your decision he gave you free will to come to him as you are you don't have to do anything but except the freedom he is giving you through his sacrifice accept him today don't wait he loves you with every fiber of his being a shed his blood for you accept Jesus Christ as your lord and savior do it today tomorrow he might return

Feb 3rd Jesus doesn't forget, He will never forget you, He will never leave you or forsake you, never is forever, for eternity, He didn't forget you on the cross, Jesus Christ did not pick and choice which sins He was going to die for, He died for all sins, Jesus's promises do not only apply to certain people, they belong to all , all that accept The Only Begotten Son of God as their Savior and Lord, you see Jesus will not forsake you, the person doing the forsaking is you, you have a part to play in this relationship, you must choose, why , because you can't serve two masters, and you do serve a master, Jesus said you will hate the one and love the other, make the choice to serve the only risen Lord, if you have not make Jesus Christ your Lord today, rejoice in the Truth that you are saved and have a home for eternity with Him

Feb 4th Who in this world has given up everything that they possessed for you, the answer is Christ, but He wasn't, but He was, 100% man, born of a virgin, live 33 years, and died the death of a thief, 100% man, and now, 100% God, after death He was resurrected by His and our Heavenly Father, Jesus had 100% completed the will of His Father which was to prepare a Way for you and Me to return to fellowship with our Creator, Satan knew the consequences of sin when he enticed Eve to eat of the tree, he was already starting His walk to the bottomless pit, what He didn't know was that the only begotten Son of God would pay our wage of sin death, yes you earned it, thank Jesus Christ that He paid it, there is only one Way to the Father and that is through the Son

Feb 5th Secure your home in paradise, be sure of eternity, don't just guess, there is only one way to insure all three are fact, follow the Truth not a lie, Jesus Christ said I am the Truth, its not a guessing game when you choose to follow Jesus, when you accept Him as Lord and Savior you are accepting fact, you have accepted the only Way back to our Heavenly Father, the one and only Way, have no doubt as to the last stop for your eternal life, have no doubt that tonight you will join Jesus in paradise, He has prepared a room for you, that room is vacant, but when you turn to Jesus Christ there is no vacancy, that room is yours, let your heart be your guide, Jesus holds that key also, all is His, be assured of victory, and victory comes through Jesus Christ

Feb 6th It doesn't matter where you are at or what you are doing, if Jesus knocks open the door, things will begin to change, circumstances that you have found no resolutions to will suddenly be resolved, with Jesus Christ you will find ways that you have never seen, Jesus Christ said He is the Way, He is coming back to take us to paradise, once you accept Jesus the process of renewal begins immediately through His Spirit, showing you the right Way not the wrong way, begin a new life today accept the only begotten Son of God as your Lord and Savior, accept Jesus Christ and secure a new beginning, as you are, Jesus will do the cleansing through His blood

Feb 7th Everyone is in a rush, they want immediate satisfaction, immediate satisfaction usually doesn't last, an instant relationship doesn't usually last, there is a with you, you need to choose a relationship with Him, this relationship with Jesus is with your heart, your heart tells the truth, to just say I want a relationship is not enough, this relationship with Jesus Christ is a yearning, a truth that comes from your heart, then when your heart cries out to Jesus will this eternal relationship begin, with Jesus all things are possible, with Jesus even the things that you have hidden will be revealed and cleansed, you will have a friend in Jesus and oh what a friend relationship that does last though, this relationship is guaranteed to last through eternity, that relationship is with the Son of God, Jesus has chosen a relationship He is

Feb 8th Everyone has an agenda, this church has a specialty, we dance more here we sing more there, there is only one agenda, there is only one way, that Way is the Way the Truth and the Life, Jesus has done all, He said it is finished, understand what the Church is, understand who is the Head of the Church, know who you are dancing for, know who you are singing for, it is not the body it is the Head, church is not a one hour show that happens once a week, it is a relationship that last all day, every day, sing for Jesus, dance for Jesus, David danced and sang for the Lord not the people, everything we do is to magnify Jesus Christ, through Jesus we magnify The Father, The Son, and The Holy Spirit, the agenda has a name it is Jesus Christ

Feb 9th Our God is an awesome God, He has the power to create or destroy, and He still waits on a decision from you, you who were created by Him, you who He sacrificed His only living Son for, knowing that Jesus Christ sacrifice would not be accepted by all, who are we to try such power, there is only one reason we live, love, an undying love for you and me , the created, our Father who is in Heaven, He cried at the sacrifice of His only begotten Son, and He cries at the loss of one of us just as hard, all will not choose to be washed in the cleansing blood of Jesus, some will want to retain the sins they have, some will choose a second death because the scales never fell from there eyes, accept Jesus Christ today, right now, and the scales will fall and you will see the reality of life forever with our Lord and Savior Jesus Christ

Feb 10th God designed us for perfection therefore we were perfect, in the garden satan flawed our perfection through sin, satan, through this act, pulled us down to his level, thinking there was no return for us to perfection, that he had once again flawed God's creation, the devil knows of Jesus Christ, he also knows there is no forgiveness of sin for him, he knows that forgiveness of sin is only for man, this gift of salvation, a return to God's grace's is given to us through the sacrifice of His only begotten Son, and His name is Jesus, through His blood our sins are washed away, forever, the devil deceives you into thinking you are not good enough, and you alone are not, but, through Jesus you are, you are perfected once again, you can return to Heaven and become reunited with our Father, His love lifted me His love will lift you

Feb 11th Share your love for Jesus, this is why they call the bible the living word of God, He is not a book to be put on a shelf, Jesus is not a history book, Both are alive, Both are living, Their words do not change, there truths are everlasting, praise our Saviors name aloud, praise our Father Abba aloud, your relationship with Jesus Christ was not complete when you accepted Him as Lord, your relationship with Jesus Christ is continuous and forever, the Holy Spirit will guide and teach you, direct you and lead you to our Father our Creator, Jesus said His will be done, it applies to you too, His will for you is to accept His only begotten Son as your Lord and Savior, to accept His gift of rejuvenation His Son provides, no one goes to the Father but through His Son, praise Their Holy names

Feb 12th Our God, who is an awesome God, does not ask you to find Him, He seeks you out, He takes a personal touch with you, your circumstances are not all the same and His loving touch is not the same, His relationship is personal to each and everyone of us, God's guidance for us helps in defining the relationship, He does not leave us blind, He explains all and the reason for all, He sent His Son Jesus Christ to clear the way to His throne of all obstacles for us, He sent His Holy Spirit to guide us, teach us, and pray for us when are not capable to pray for ourselves, and He sends angels to intervene when His personal touch needs to be felt, you are not alone, you never have been alone, open your eyes to the awesome power of our God, to the awesome power of His Son Jesus Christ, and to the awesome power of His Holy Spirit, All have one agenda, you, He will never forsake you or leave you

God Made You

Feb 13th So many people are lost, lost to reality, lost to the Truth, they do not deny the king of lies but they will deny the very existence of the King of Kings, they have no idea of the future, so many claim to know and no nothing, they lack the wisdom of the very words of God, they do not see the dread that is just ahead, Jesus Christ said if you deny me Iv will deny you to the Father, in fact He will say I never knew you, everyone will stand before the King of Kings Lord of Lords, it will be to late to accept Him on the day of judgement, accept Him today, do not continue to let satan deceive you, know the Truth and you will know the Way and the Life, Jesus Christ is all encompassing, He will not forsake you, satan has no such guarantee other than the bottomless pit, shun him and he will flee, open your eyes to the Light

Feb 15th Please understand, this relationship with our Savior Jesus Christ is a total commitment, Jesus said you can not serve two masters and you can't, this relationship is not a hello and goodbye run into each other in the street type of relationship, the bible compares this relationship to a marriage, not an earthly marriage but a whole hearted devoted Heavenly marriage, you cannot believe half of what is said, commit all or nothing, this is why Jesus can say He never knew you, you never gave all, He gave all to you even to death, this world will not last, but our transfigured spiritual bodies will, let Jesus inspire you, yes, you need to allow it, Jesus Christ will not force Himself on you, He wants a relationship with you but you must want a relationship with Him, He will wait as long as the Father allows, find Jesus and believe on Him

Feb 16th God has no bias except sin, He who created all things created you, there is no difference between us in His eyes, the difference is in our eyes, any falling away is done by you, so Jesus waits on you, the King of Kings Lord of Lords waits on you, you want freedom God gives you freedom, man takes away your freedoms to conform to the standards they set, man tries to control all they can, guess what, man can't control your heart, Jesus said I will give you a new heart, the Holy Spirit will teach us the reality of life, that reality is Jesus Christ, that reality is what He did to bring you back into the fold, what He did to bring you into green pastures, what He did so you could lie down beside still waters, what Jesus did for you and me could not have been done by anyone else, Jesus is the answer because He controls everything

Feb 17th If we would simple open our eyes to creation you would not doubt that there is a Creator, if you open your eyes you would not doubt the word of God Our Creator, if you open your eyes to the word of God you would not doubt His only begotten Son Jesus Christ, close your eyes to the world and open your eyes to the Truth, this world will end and a new one begins, it is hard to open your eyes to the Truth when you believe the lies of this world, pray and your Redeemer will hear you, and when Jesus hears you He will talk with His Father, and, and as your eyes are opened to the Truth you will be able to begin a life of renewal though the Trinity, you will be able to discern the lies of this world and see the Truths of the Trinity

Feb 18th You must want a relationship with Jesus, you must seek after Him, He is not illusive, He is waiting for you to look His way, are you looking in all the wrong places, try looking in your heart, what does your heart hold, if it is still holding the world there is no room for Jesus Christ, you can not serve two masters, it is not peer pressure it is world pressure, Jesus Christ has already conquered this world, He has lived, died, and been resurrected back to the throne of our Father, come as you are and let Jesus cleanse that heart and begin a new life in you, the only friend that can save you is Jesus Christ, and yes oh what a Friend we have in Jesus

Feb 19th The world wants us to embrace the ungodly, accept people for who they are, don't judge, I do not judge, the judgement has been made for me in the very words of God, is it not an abomination in the eyes of God, even if we look the other way, well were not suppose to judge, pray then, pray for the Lords will to be done, pray for His intervention, He has already sent His Son to intervene and change lives, to turn hearts of stone to hearts of flesh, all the abominations we see to day all rolls up to one thing, people do not recognize the power of our Lord Jesus Christ , so many don't know Him and so many don't care to know Him, no wonder Noah was the only one to make it through the flood, pray, pray to our sovereign Lord, our Redeemer, our Savior, pray for His intervention in all these lost peoples life

Feb 20th Don't forsake the gift of Jesus Christ anymore, he said he wouldn't forsake you or Leave you, you will never leave him unless you want to, so many don't believe because they don't know, so many don't believe because they choose not to, Jesus Christ laid down his life for yours so you can return to heaven, don't let this precious gift go unclaimed, this is the grace that we all need, this grace that he gives, come As You Are this gift is free as his love is free

Feb 21st Why are you called Christian, because every day you grow closer and closer to Jesus, you act more and more like Christ, one thing Jesus Christ taught us is to pray, not once or twice but diligently, so pray, pray for the morality of this world, pray our Father who art in Heaven watches over His children, Jesus insures that He will always be with us, pray that He walks with you and if Jesus Christ is walking with you, you are walking the walk not just talking the talk, so pray for His healing Hand to bring peace for His children, it may rain on us as well but the rain is full of His Grace for those that believe, so pray continuously for His will to be done, don't accept this world because once you have accepted Jesus Christ as your Lord and Savior you are no longer part of this world, so pray

Feb 22nd What are you thinking about today, what was your first thought, when do you first talk with God, before or after you need Him, they persecute our talk with Jesus because they do not converse with Jesus at all, we as Christians have a relationship with our Lord and Savior, people that ridicule that talk have no relationship with Jesus Christ, Jesus said I was persecuted and so will you, Jesus Christ has shown us everything including the persecution, talk, walk, run, sleep, do everything with Jesus, those that ridicule and persecute Christians will never understand the Truth until they accept the Truth which is Jesus Christ, so, in not knowing their arrogance will come out against you and their arrogance will come out against Him, King of Kings Lord of Lords, and yes, as Jesus plainly pointed out, if you are not for Him you will be against Him

Feb 23rd How many obstacles are there between you and God, how big is the obstacle between you and God, who is in control of the obstacles between you and God, are, if you never said a word your prayer would make it to God, and when you accept Jesus Christ as your Lord and Savior your prayers will be hand delivered, there is only one obstacle between you and God, it's you, how big is obstacles, you the only begotten Son of God becomes your voice, and when the hurt is so deep the Holy Spirit will continue your prayers when you can't, once you open your heart to Jesus Christ, your heart is opened to the entire Trinity, all of Their love embraces you, your talk with Jesus will become a walk with Jesus, if He is for you who can be against you the obstacle between you and God, as big as you make it, and who

Feb 24th Jesus Christ was asked when will you return, Jesus said there will be signs, Our Creator does not leave us blind to future events, He does not leave us blind to current events either, open your eyes, the question is are you opening your eyes with a heart of stone or a heart of flesh, if you have not accepted Jesus Christ as your Lord and Savior is in control of these, you are looking at events with scales over your eyes, Jesus said these things will happen, He did not say they might happen, prepare your heart for eternity through Jesus because of the actions of Jesus, politics belong to ceasar, reality belongs to our risen Lord, one is a lie, the other is all Truth, Truth is one of the names of our King Jesus Christ, the only begotten Son of God

Feb 26th Every time you move there is a purpose, nothing is random, this is how unique God has made us, and as individuals God loves us individually and Jesus Christ loves us individually, God said you would not be tempted beyond what you could stand and that there will always be an escape, there is an escape from this carnal world, this escape has a name Jesus Christ, the Way, the Truth, and the Life, Jesus is all encompassing, there is no point in your life He does not see and foresee, He said He would never leave us nor forsake us, and yes even through death to life, He will walk you through the valley of death, He has already been there and conquered it, because of Him you will be triumphant also, you will live beyond the grave in eternity with Jesus Christ, in eternity with Abba Father, in eternity with the Holy Spirit, if you don't know Jesus Christ today talk with Him He will answer you and get to know Him, if you already know Jesus Christ as your Lord and Savior then praise His Holy name, through Him you will be born again

Feb 27th Isn't it wonderful that God waits on us, we often say we will get to it but let me finish this first, are we not really saying just this one last sin, this world holds nothing that releases us from bondage, but, Heaven holds the key, Jesus Christ waits on you, you have until He returns, He waits on you, He does hold the key to the bottomless pit, accept Jesus as your Lord and Savior and you will be set free from the bondage this world holds against you, the false accuser has no power over our Risen Savior, but , our Risen Savior Jesus Christ holds all the power, make Jesus your King today and glorify His name

Feb 28th If you listen you will hear the words of God, He will give you options that steer you away from places or things that may test your faith in Jesus Christ, if you listen to the Holy Spirit instead of the spirit of the world you will find blessings instead of reasons to repent and ask for forgiveness, this is one of the ways that our lives are influenced by the Holy Spirit, it is very true that Jesus Christ will not forsake us or leave us, don't let the world influence you, instead listen to the Holy Spirit, know that you belong to the Kingdom of God and through His power you will always be blessed in the end if you listen and let Him guide your way and not the world

Mar 1st Why do so many people ask if the country should turn back to God, if you Know God, if you know Jesus Christ His Son, if you know the Holy Spirit, you would not even ask that question, to know Him is to love Him and once you know Him you will never want to let Him go, God certainly would not let you slip from His hands, accept Jesus Christ our Lord and Savior for who He is , repent , and return triumphant through Him and you will know the glory and the peace of being a child of God once more, so yes we do need to turn to God and repent, all is forgiven through the sacrifice of His only begotten Son, all has been accomplished for you. the you part is what seals the deal, eternity is free, a life with Jesus Christ is the reward from Him to you, He is all Truth and all Love

Mar 2nd Who's power are you relying on, if you see no help from the world, who's power are you relying on, you are relying on yourself, if this is where you stand in life you are standing alone, help is watching, crying because you do not know the Truth, accept Jesus Christ and help will always be available to you. you will never be alone again, Jesus Christ power will become your power, His strength will become your strength, mountains will begin to shrink to a size you can negotiate and easily step over, all of this begins to happen because the Creator of all things is with you, the word of God says with man nothing is possible but with God all things are possible, Jesus is the Way, the Truth, and the Life, no one goes to the Father but through Him

Mar 3rd There is always a solution, one is temporary and one is permanent, which one do you choose, if you are still a part of the world you will always choose the temporary one, if you want a permanent solution to everything all you need to do is choose Jesus Christ, the hard part is when you choose Jesus Christ this needs to be a permanent decision, a heartfelt decision, a decision of repentance, but if you haven't felt our Heavenly Fathers tug of your heart to find His only begotten Son and to find Him for a relationship of love you will always be stuck on temporary, everything you see is temporary until you see Jesus, until you pray with Jesus, until you become reliant on Jesus Christ, until that relationship becomes permanent, so find that permanent answer to a temporary problem, find and accept Jesus Christ as your Savior and Lord

Mar 4th So many people profess a knowledge of nothing, they claim no allegiance to anything, and many of these people have a platform that reaches around the world, the deceiver is hard at work, satans message is reaching around the world and many of the messengers of Jesus Christ haven't noticed, satan will attempt to pass himself off as God, He studies the word of God daily, do you? know the word of God, satan cannot mimic the fullness of Jesus Christ, remember a mirror image is not the image, the Holy Spirit will give you the gift of discernment, pray for this gift' open your eyes to the deception that is this world, accept Jesus Christ and receive His perfection not the imperfection of the devil

Mar 5th Don't give up on Jesus Christ, He will never give up on you, if on the final day of your life you realize that the truth is the Truth and your heart opens up to the King of Kings Lord of Lords, He will wash you and cleanse you of your sins and accept you as you have accepted Him, but why wait for perfection till the end, why not accept Jesus Christ today, today may even be your final day, it may be your final hour, it may be your final second, but no matter the time of day Jesus knocks, just open the door and let Him in, the day you embrace Jesus Christ is the day you will realize why you were even born, why you were even created by God, our Father who is in Heaven, the scales will drop from your eyes and you will not only see with your eyes but you will also see with your heart, that day will be the day you are reborn

Mar 6th Where is your jesus, who is your personal jesus, if you don't know who he is or where he is, you do not know Jesus Christ, pray to the real Jesus and He will answer, He will answer where no other jesus can, in your heart, don't be fooled there is only one risen Savior and that is Jesus Christ the only begotten Son of God, there are many sons of God but there is only one begotten Son of God, there is only one Heir and that is Jesus the Messiah, satan is the greatest deceiver you will ever come against, and you will be fooled without help, that help is Jesus, that hope is the Holy Spirit that comes to you when you have accepted Jesus Christ as your Lord and King, Jesus is above all kings and all lords, The Real Jesus can be yours, pray for His deliverance

Mar 8th Pray and wait, pray and wait, pray and wait, don't give up, pray that you are able to see or you're able to hear the answer to your prayer, is there anything in your way, is your heart open to receive Jesus Christ, if you are not for the Him, you are against Him, no matter pray, all of us were His enemy at one time, no matter Jesus still was crucified, He was crucified for everything we did and nothing He did, while we were still enemies He died and paid for our release, He died so we could return to our Father, He died so we could receive forgiveness for all of our sins, His blood washed us clean, are you washed clean, no matter, Jesus said come as you are, receive Him and receive a new life, so pray

Mar 9th What is faith without works, this work is something you do out of love not out of necessity, this work is something you do because it is what our Lord and Savior Jesus Christ would do, help each other and pray for your enemies, Jesus Christ set the examples, He Truly talked the talk and walked the walk, it is not what would Jesus do, it is what Jesus has already done, on the cross He said it is finished, He has proven that He is worthy through the grace He has shown us, are you worthy of Him through the faith you show, accept Jesus Christ, be cleansed by His blood, begin to walk in faith, don't just walk

Mar 10th Every time you think of Jesus today, remember He thought of you first, God says He knew you in the womb, guess what Jesus has been waiting for just that long, He will wait your whole life, He waits on you, waits for you to turn to Him and embrace Him, slow down enough today to hear His voice, a voice that has been calling out to you every day of your life, stop and listen and His voice will be heard as the noise of this world fades into the background, you will find the relationship that you have lacked and always wanted, embrace Jesus Christ as your Lord and Savior and you will be reborn into His kingdom, your spiritual eye will begin to open to the reality of this world and to a Savior that gave up everything for you and His Father, He gave up everything so you could live the life you were created to live not the life the world blinded you with, and you will say I was blind but now I see

Mar 11th Day by day you live, Jesus said you don't know what tomorrow will bring, and you can't change yesterday, but there is an assurance you can have every day, that assurance is the Trinity, our Father, His son Jesus Christ, and the Holy Spirit, They are with you always, They have accepted you if you have accepted Them, They are willing to accept you even if you haven't accepted them, but first in your step to eternity is Jesus Christ, know in your heart that what He has done is True, then accept Jesus Christ and the rest of the Trinity will accept you and all Three will become part of your everyday, but first Jesus, no one goes to the Father except thru the Son

Mar 12th Do we know how to humble ourselves, when you are praying where do your prayers go, to Jesus, to our Father who art in Heaven, to the throne of God, do you have any humility, if you don't your prayers don't either, Jesus said if you humble yourself and pray He would hear, if you are petitioning a King , if you are petitioning a Lord, go to Him with humility, if you will humble yourself and change, if you will humble yourself, don't go to the throne with pride unless it is pride in Jesus Christ, expect an audience with a King because that is where you and your prayers are received, humble yourself and Jesus will hear from above

Mar 13th We prepare for everything, we prepare for work, we prepare for sleep, we prepare for anything and everything, sometimes our preparations take a few minutes sometimes they take days, well there is one thing that takes no preparation at all, the preparation has already been accomplished for you, all you need to do is make a decision about eternity and where you want to spend it, make no decision and spend it in the bottomless pit of despair, so what is this decision, a decision to accept Jesus Christ for what He is, King of Kings Lord of Lords, a decision to accept Jesus for who He is, the only begotten Son of God, and a decision to accept Him for what He did, died on a cross for your sins, conquered death and set the captives free, and was resurrected back to our Father in Heaven right hand side in the very Throne room of God, just one all-encompassing decision on your everlasting future, life or a second death

Mar 14th There are many emotions here on this earth, there are many things that bring these emotions to the front and show in many different ways, emotions that cause hurt, anger that causes death and sorrow and tears, these emotions are not just for a few, Jesus said what happens to one will happen to all, there is a place that you can go for relief and comfort, that place is into the very arms of Jesus, He will take us to a new Heaven and a new Earth, there there will be no tears or sorrow, there there will be no death, there we will be with the King of Kings, Lord of Lords, there we will be in the loving arms of God

Mar 15th It is simple today, Jesus said come to Him, the problem is the lies of satan that have blinded the eyes of the captives, those of us that know the Truth needs to tell of the power and glory of Jesus Christ, don't worry of the reactions of your so called friends, worry what Jesus will tell you, Jesus said if you deny Him He will deny you, so many people denounce Jesus Christ on a worldwide stage, they are blind they cannot see, but they can hear, tell them of your Lord and Savior, share the good news of the Gospel, don't keep it hidden in your heart, tell the captives of Jesus Christ, we were all captives to a lie at one time, share Jesus with everyone, share the Truth

Mar 16th Jesus has always been, and you have always been on His mind, His love is you, everything He has ever done is for you and because of you, some deny this but yes He even talks to you, are your eyes open to His voice, are your ears open to His voice, His answers come when you seek Him, do you expect an answer, are you looking and listening for an answer, is your heart open to Jesus Christ, the only begotten Son of God, Jesus does answer, you have to be receptive to His voice, He said He would never leave you or forsake you, you must open the door and let Him in, Jesus is offering you a relationship with the Trinity, you must choose Him, He has already chosen you

Mar 17th Our Father who is in Heaven has given us a guide to life, a book that has all the answers, some call it the Holy Bible, others call it the Word of God, and still people wonder why is this happening or why is that happening, the future has been told by God Himself, you don't need to go to a fortune teller or a palm reader, if you want to know what the future holds as it concerns' the world or just you all you have to do is study the words of God, of course without being complete you will never understand the Truth, first open your hearts door to Jesus Christ, a Son provided by a Father to save us who cannot save ourselves, once you know Jesus as your Savior and Lord then the Holy Spirit will dwell with you and teach you Gods word, all is provided to you once you become a child of God

Mar 18th Is the will of God even sought, not without prayer, we can pray for His will, we as His children can pray to our Father Abba, some do not know nor notice our Father, our Lord and Savior Jesus Christ, nor ever felt the loving nudge of the Holy Spirit, they deny that my Savior Jesus answer prayers, they deny that He even has a voice, praise God today that I, that we as children of God hear our Lord's words, that He loves us enough to answer us personally, yes our vice president talks with and hears Jesus's voice, don't fault those that don't know, confess to those that don't know, don't condemn them, pray for them, we have a great commission, spread the good news of the Gospel of Jesus Christ

Mar 19th People are looking for love, to have love you first must have a relationship, to have love you must have an understanding of the person or object you love, Jesus said the love of money is the root of all evil, this love is one sided and gives you nothing eternal, this type of love closes your eyes and your heart, there is a love that is fulfilling beyond any expectation, this love is agape love, this love is the love that Jesus Christ has for you, a type of love that will never leave you or forsake you, this love is defining above all other loves, seek out this relationship with our Lord and Savior and this forever love can be yours, as you realize the perfect love you are receiving you will began to realize that this love was the love you really always looked for, this fulfilling love of Jesus Christ

Mar 20th What did our Creator give us from the beginning, He gave us responsibility for of all of His creation, one part of that creation He gave us responsibility for was a creation in His own image, you, me, man was created in the image of our Father who is in Heaven, we failed miserable, the influences of the father of lies has distorted the Truth and we believed him, oh why didn't our Creator leave a guide, He did, at first it was in the form of prophets, men that God spoke thru, now it is in the form a book which holds all His words for instruction, still we could not, so He sent us a Savior in the form of His only begotten Son, Jesus Christ, with Jesus all is forgiven, with Jesus a teacher of the word of God comes to us in the form of the Holy Spirit, with Jesus Christ we cannot fail, without Him we will fail miserable, the one and only answer is Jesus Christ

God Made You

Mar 21st They say the Bible is a mystery, they say they solved a portion, they make shows to entertain about it as if it is a fantasy, all of this is done for the love of money, they exploit even the words of God, the Bible is not a mystery if you reach out to the one that wrote it, if you know the son Jesus Christ you know the Author, if you know Jesus Christ as your Lord and Savior you have the one that will break all the so called codes, you have the Holy Spirit, all exploitation of the Word of God is thrown to the wayside when you know the Fathers Son Jesus Christ, knowing the Truth will set you free, Jesus said I am the Way, the Truth, and the Life, no one goes to the Father but through Me, mystery solved. code broke, question answered, all of this is wrapped up in the only begotten Son of God, Jesus Christ

Mar 22nd Let Gods blessings flow, how many times do we overlook a blessing, every day, every single day is a blessing, you are a blessing, you are a deliverer of Gods blessings, you are an instrument of the Great I Am, be a blessing, look for others to be a blessing to you, if we all shared the blessing of love there would not be chaos in the world today, but all of us are not an instrument of God some have chosen to be an instrument of evil for their king the father of lies, but if you are a child of the One True God then be the blessing you are meant to be, share the love you have for Jesus Christ our Lord and King, share the Way the Truth and the Life, share His love and be the blessing you are meant to be, the adversary wants you to think you are nothing, Jesus wants you to know the blessing you are, so be that blessing to someone today

Mar 23rd What are people waiting on, are they so blinded by the creation that they can't see the Creator, man wants to dress up the package, make it shiny and beautiful, but inside it is still filthy and ugly, the decay and rot of the world is still there, the lies of satan still hide the Truth, if you want a package transformed make it a Temple, yes the package is your body and when you accept Jesus Christ as your Redeemer your body becomes a Temple for His Spirit to reside in, your heart changes from stone to flesh and then a Heavenly smile shows through as the world is left behind and you begin a relationship with Heaven, you begin a relationship with the Creator instead of the created, the package becomes beautiful inside and out, it no longer hides the Truth

Mar 24th No matter how hard you try there are some things that you cannot prepare for, many people will tell you your life is in your hands, and to some extent it is, you can choose to remain blind to the reality of Jesus Christ and continue with the up and downs of this life, or you can prepare for your eternal life after this one, you can think you can pay the price for your sins yourself, or you can accept the all cleansing blood of the Lamb of God who has paid the price that you will never be able to pay , the price for your sins can only be paid by the only begotten Son of our Father who art in Heaven, who sent His Son to earth to set the captives free and secure your future in Paradise, or you can simply exchange one hell for another, sure you can find some happiness on earth in these bodies of clay, or you can have an eternal Happiness in a transfigured body provided by our Father Abba and His Son Jesus and His Spirit, all of which took part in the first creation, and the Three will also create the New Heaven and the New Earth, you will choose it is your choice

Mar 25th If you only believe, you know the history, some just say it is a good read, to people that say that the bible is just a good read, it is, to those that have faith, to those that know the Truth, to those that have a relationship with Gods only begotten Son, to those like Saul who have had the scales removed from their eyes through the love of our Lord and Savior, to the ones that have knelt and cried as you felt the Grace of a Holy Spirit embrace, Jesus Christ said I Am the Truth, I Am the Way, I Am the Life, to those that know the Truth, it is true, to those that have not accepted the Truth, to those that can't see the Way because of the scales of the world. To those that don't listen with their hearts, it is still true, their denial of factual history only leads to a second death, Jesus said He came to set the captives free, the door to your cell is unlocked, turn the handle and walk into the loving embrace of our Lord and Savior Jesus Christ, don't believe the lies of the father of lies anymore

Mar 26th Yea though I walk thru the valley of death, Jesus Christ has already been there, I will fear no evil, Jesus Christ has already conquered it, thy rod and thy staff will comfort me, Jesus Christ leads all those that have accepted Him for the Truth, our Lord and Savior is with us all the way to the Throne of God, He is there to greet us when we arrive, once you invite Jesus into your life He is with you always, He said He would not leave you nor forsake you, this is a personal promise from our King, all was given into His hands, Truly if He is for us who can be against us, satan himself ask permission to look our way, we are children of God and we serve a Risen Savior, don't doubt that you are special, Jesus Christ has made you special, serve your King Jesus Christ by serving others, follow His example, you are chosen

Mar 27th We were created in the image of God, and we were perfect, everything was good, it is amazing that everything can be controlled by diet, and your environment, there was no disease until disease met us in the Garden, God knew exactly what we needed, and He can provide all, you want perfection go to God, if you want imperfection go to man, God is always 100%, man have flaws that cannot be corrected but by an all loving Lord and Savior, a Savior named Jesus Christ, a Savior that gave all, so you can choose to rely on perfection or you will choose to rely on imperfection, Jesus said you cannot serve two masters, if you are a child of God you will serve God, but if you are a child of the flesh you will serve the flesh and satan, satan has an agenda for you and his agenda is a lie, rely on the Truth rely on Jesus

Mar 28th You don't have to run everywhere to find acceptance, you don't have to run everywhere to find love, give your love to Jesus and He will return with His love in abundance, He will accept you as you are, He wants you to come to Him as you are, He knows what is in your heart and has accepted you, Jesus said He would never leave you His love is forever, Jesus said He would never forsake you, with Jesus your name will never be forgotten, serve Jesus where you are treasured forever, not man who will neglect you on a whim, Jesus wants you, He is the only one that paid the price of redemption for you, a price you could never pay, He paid, He was the only one capable

God Made You

Mar 29th Everybody says give this a chance give that a chance, you can deal in chances or you can know for certain, the world is full of chances, Jesus is full of certainties, there are no might's or maybes, Jesus Christ is all Truth, and only deals in Truths, there is no sleight of hand tricks in His arsenal, He is not a magician, He is a King, He is a Lord, He is a Savior, He is the only begotten Son of God, He has authority to do all because all was given into His hands, all loving and all powerful, be still and know, know that He is King of Kings Lord of Lords, let Jesus refresh your life with His love, He said He would not forsake you or leave you, don't forsake Him or leave Him, deal in the worlds game of chance or be assured through the actions of Jesus Christ and the reality of His everlasting love

Mar 30th Jesus said you cannot serve two masters, and Jesus is right, talk with Him when you arise from your rest, let Him start your day out right and direct your path, it is so easy to get lost, or distracted throughout the day without His presence in your life, He gave an example of how to live, He gave an example of how to serve, everything is not what it seems, sometimes misdirection is intentional so you take your eyes of God, the Holy Spirit will help, Jesus will help, when you are under attack, listen and you will hear the voices of the Trinity and the feel the love They have for you, the world is not King of Kings, Jesus is, the world is not Lord of Lords, Jesus is, there is only one way to Salvation and that's thru our Redeemer Jesus Christ, not the world

Mar 31st If you know Jesus, you can see Jesus , if you know Jesus you can hear Jesus, if you know Jesus, you can touch Jesus, if you know Jesus you can serve like Jesus, if you don't know Jesus Christ, how could you ever be able to see, hear, or touch Him, if you want to talk to an audience you have to know your audience, the only way to know a Christian is to know who they serve, and who they serve is the only begotten Son of God, the only one that paid a price He did not owe, the first resurrected from death back to Heaven, a King, a Lord, a Savior, a friend who gave His life for me, a Redeemer, to actually know Jesus is to love Jesus, don't hide His light in your heart tell others, show others His light, as timothy said faith without works is dead

Apr 1st What is in your heart, you know if Jesus can say rather He knew you or not, you can tell if a person is telling the truth or a lie, the Holy Spirit knows what is in your heart, given discernment we as Christians know what is really in some ones heart, Jesus said if you are not for Him you are against Him, Jesus knows what is in the heart, some people portray themselves a certain way for the love of money, all the tools you need is given to you from the Throne of God, God, Jesus, and the Holy Spirit Have provided the written word of who they are and what they have done for you, when you know Jesus Christ a personal teacher in the Holy Spirit is given to you to discern and understand Who we serve and why we serve a Risen Savior, it has nothing to do with the mind, it has everything to do with the heart, with your mind you can talk the talk, only with your heart can you walk the walk, Jesus has walked the walk, He is deserving of all praise

Apr 2nd Open your eyes and ask yourself why is Christianity the most persecuted relationship in the world, the world will deny Jesus Christ in one breath and slander who He is in the next breath, and still Jesus will forgive, His love for us is beyond measurement, you spew the most vile remarks and yet when you truly repent to Him He forgives, all power was given to Him, who has this authority, our Creator, our Father who art in Heaven, there is nothing further you can do to Jesus, He has conquered life as a man, and went on to conquer death, the world could not hold Him, He has risen, and thru Jesus you too can overcome, He is the Way the only Way

Apr 3rd In no way are you on the same level as Jesus Christ, His humility seems to make some people assume that they too are, His silence gives them the impression they have a right to interpret what He has said, don't let them deceive you and get you caught up in their lies, Jesus Christ Himself has or will provide you with a Comforter, a Teacher, a piece of His very being, Jesus Christ has provided, He has provided you with the Holy Spirit, if you have chosen Him as your Lord and Savior, the Holy Spirit will teach you the words of our Creators, He will teach you, Jesus said He would not leave you alone and as He said He did, rely on the one all power has been given, not the one that only deceives, rely on Jesus Christ

Apr 4th Jesus is conquering death, Jesus has already paid the price for your sins, He said the wagers of sin is death, tomorrow He will begin His ascension back to the Father, before He returns there will be plenty of eyewitnesses to His resurrection, yes it is fact, there were more than three witnesses, everything Jesus did throughout His life was biblical, Jesus lived the words of His Father Abba, Jesus did what His Father and our Father Asked Him, Jesus said as He prayed to His Father your will be done not mine, God has left nothing in the dark, all He is, stands in the light, His words are true, Jesus Christ words are true, hold to them and receive the love of God, agape love, and thirst no more, through the actions of the Son you are now able to go to the Father

Apr 5th After Jesus returned from the grave many people saw Him, He had finished paying for our sins and yet He did not leave us, He brought captives back with Him, also a testament to what He had done, everything Jesus Christ did or does in the light, He is not hidden from those that seek Him, so many, even some that say they know Him do not, they deceive their real intent, to serve the father of lies, that is why the Holy Spirit attends to us always, to keep the deceptions of the world from corrupting us, to show us the lies that barrage us daily, satan does not stop, his lies are never ceasing, his attempts to deceive are non-stop, seek Jesus and you will find Him, when you find Him and know Him and accept Him for your Lord and Savior, you also will be a captive set free

Apr 6th Easter isn't for another year, as this day draws to an end, is Jesus's memory fading as well, oh well we can keep it together for another year, oh we have Christmas in between, let me tell you of our Risen Lord, Lord of Lords, King of Kings, Savior, He has not forgotten you, as a matter of fact what He did for us, paying a price we could not pay, is for every second of every day of every year you will ever live, He said He would never forsake you or leave you, are you going to forsake Him until another Holy Day, He will still love you as if you had never missed a second with Him ,He Has not missed a second with you, even if it was only waiting for you to look His way again, if you don't know Jesus as your Savior and Lord look His way and begin to know His love for you, when you do you will want to spend eternity with Him

Apr 7th Jesus gave us examples on how to live, and He hid nothing from us, He said because I was persecuted so will you be persecuted, and so we are, praise the Apr 8th Lord He did not run from the Cross, He paid the price for our redemption, don't be so blind as to not see that we belong to the Kingdom of the Lord, daily Christianity is attacked and the religions of the world are presented in a way that says they are alternatives to Glory, they are not, Jesus said I Am the Way, I Am the Truth, I Am the Life, no one goes to the Father but through Me, we were all created in the image of God, the father of lies, the deceiver, the false accuser, mimics the Glory of Heaven, what he portrays to you is a lie, accept a Real King, accept the only King, accept Jesus Christ as your Lord and Savior and the scales will fall from your eyes and you will see

Apr 9th Your heart tells the truth, nothing is hidden, you may be able to hide the contents from man but you can't hide the contents from God the Father or Jesus His Son, they know the real you, not the you you show to the world, and they still love you with an everlasting love, when Jesus occupies your heart He begins to mend all the hurts no one knows about, He begins a process of renewal through love, Jesus cares, He even knows the hurts that you have hidden so deep that you have forgotten them, His Spirit stays with you always, and His Spirit prays for you when you cant find the words, you do have a true friend in Jesus and you are His number one concern, who can be against you if

Jesus is for you, remember wake up with prayer, put on the full armor of God, don't go back out into the world without it

Apr 10th You said it rains on the just and unjust, Your Son is my umbrella, He is my Comforter in a storm, He can calm a raging sea, through Jesus you are protected, He paid the price for sin for the whole world, and still the world does not notice or care, the world does not know Jesus Christ, Jesus is everything the world is not, the world demands, Jesus, King of Kings gives, His life being one, paying a price that we could never pay, so now because of the sacrifice of Jesus Christ we can run to Gods mountain instead of away, because of Jesus we can have a relationship with the Alpha and Omega, the Beginning and the End, through Jesus all is possible, He has given All

Apr 11th It is very simple, people say I am not deserving of the gift Jesus Christ gives me, I can't except this, I am not worthy, and you are right, you in yourself cannot add to or take away from anything in this creation, at one point we were given this world, but we failed in the beginning, well in the beginning a plan was already in progress to bring us back, the Father asked the Son if He would do this, the Son told the Father not my will but your will be done, the will of the Father was to save us, and Jesus Christ did just that, He was crucified, and died on a cross under the persecution of the ones He sought to save, He conquered death and set the captives free, He was resurrected and returned to His Father's side, through His actions you have been set free, Jesus has the keys to the cell you are in, ask and you will receive, accept the gift, accept Jesus Christ because He is the gift, the gift of life

God Made You

Apr 12th In this world you can be anything you want, you can be a leader or a follower, you can save money or spend money, you can be rich or poor, everybody you know is in a category, let me tell you something that nobody on earth can be, a Savior for everyone on earth, only one man could do this, only one man could pay a price for something He never did, it was a payment that none could pay but everyone has the opportunity to partake in the benefits of this payment, Jesus Christ made this payment, through His actions all of us have been set free, even today He sits to the right of God interceding on our behalf, this gift is free, so many have been convinced that this cannot be real, it is real, accept Jesus today and reap the benefits of His Salvation, accept Jesus today and receive His undying Love, He has conquered death, His gifts are forever

Apr 13th Everyone thinks they know what is right, everyone thinks they know the correct actions to do, the correct direction to go, only through the grace of God are you even given tomorrow, there is only one person that did everything right, everything He ever did in His life including till death, nothing broke the laws handed down through Moses, there was no sin in Him, Jesus Christ was the one and only person that could have been the perfect final sacrifice, Jesus had no sin until your sins were placed upon His shoulders to bare, He paid that price to wash your sins away, that price was death, Jesus conquered death and now holds the key to life, accept Jesus with your whole heart and he will remove you from the cell of this world and take you into His fold where you will truly lie down by still waters

Apr 14th Look around at people today and tell me that you did not know, you do not know because you choose not to know, you don't need to go any further than the bible to know the future, those that deny the Truth don't know the Truth, the Truth is Jesus Christ, persecution has been going on for a long time, denial of facts and history is real, you want the truth, you can't handle the truth, unless, unless you belong to the Truth, the Truth is Jesus Christ, accept Him and the truth will reveal itself, Jesus holds the keys to the past, present, and future, He can change you from a past sinner into a child of God, He is the key the only key, and Jesus will set you free

Apr 15th All the books in the world could not contain what Jesus Christ has accomplished, none of these accomplishments were done to glorify Himself, all that Jesus did was to Glorify His Father, Abba, and serve Him, or, it was done to save us from this world and serve us, nothing He did was for Himself or for His own edification, all Jesus ever did was serve others, all power was given Him by God our Father, His title King of Kings Lord of Lords was given to Him, the only thought of Jesus was His Father and what His Fathers will was, to save us, to purify us, to bring us back into the Fold of God, so yes He lived a sin free life, this was done so He could take on the sins of a world that did not know Him, one that in the end killed Him by crucifixion, but His life did not end there, He went on to conquer death and set the captives free, and then resurrected back to the Fathers right side to reign forever for you, to intercede for you, to love you, He accomplished all and all was given to Him, humble yourself and glorify Jesus the Son of the only living God

God Made You

Apr 16th People don't know the many names of our Lord and Savior Jesus Christ, people want to debate the undebatable, the Truth is undebatable, Jesus took part in creation, in the beginning was the Word, the Trinity are one in thought there is no difference at all, Jesus does not paraphrase, His words are the exact words of the Father, words that He received directly from the Father, all is exact Truth, there is no room for error, what One said they All said, any division in the Word of God comes from the world not the Creators of the world, satan deceives, he deceives by simple asking is that what God meant when He said, yes that is exactly what God meant because that is exactly what God said, know the Words of God they are written down in the number one best seller of all time, the word of God, the Holy bible

Apr 17th So many people claim to know the answers to life's questions, there are all kind of self-help books, all inspired by man, there is only one self-help book inspired by God, and there is only one self-help Spirit given by Jesus Christ and that is the Holy bible and the Holy Spirit, both are provided to you by a loving God, and if you search you will find the answer to all the questions of life, given to you by the authority of life, the Creator of life, His words are given to you so there is a Way to live and serve one another just as Jesus the Son of God served us, once you accept Jesus Christ as your Lord and Savior all division between an eternal life with God the Father is taken away by the Son Jesus Christ

Apr 18th After sin we became captives, captives to the world, and the world destroyed itself, we are descendants of our Creator, we are descendants of Adam, after the flood, we are all descendants of Noah, God said He would not destroy earth with water again, Jesus is going to return to subdue the nations, to subdue the world, He will conquer the world, He has already conquered death, all will become new, the old will pass away, the New Jerusalem will take the place of the old, Jesus and His Father will occupy that new city and from that Throne will flow the River of Life, Jesus conquered death, for those that accept Jesus as Lord and Savior will not fell its sting, and they will drink freely from the River, those that deny Him will not quench their thirst

Apr 19th What are you worth to the world, nothing, what are you worth to Jesus, everything, there are so many reasons for unbelief, love is the reason for belief, love for the Father, love for the Son, and love for the Holy Spirit, the world gives you a moment of happiness followed by an eternity of darkness, Jesus Christ gave you all He had to include His own life followed by an eternity of Light, Love, and Grace, don't let this second of time here on earth cause you an eternity of separation from our Father, our Creator, our true Life and Reason, we were made for fellowship with God, when He created us we were perfect, return to perfection through the gift of Jesus Christ and the help of the Holy Spirit

Apr 20th Are you willing to serve as Jesus Christ serve's you, Jesus is just as willing to die for you today as the day He did die for you, His love for you has not changed, the world is full of turbulent waters, you can find tranquility with Jesus, He will guide you to still waters, He will guide you to green pastures, people eat from the trash bin of this world and think they are satisfied, Jesus Christ gives the real satisfaction that we seek, tell the world of the eternal grace you have found in Jesus, witness for your Lord and Savior, witness of His glory, plant a seed for salvation and restoration, tell the world of Jesus Christ

Apr 21st Everything is recorded in the bible, Jesus's entire life is there, His miraculous birth to a virgin, His ministry and miracles He did during his sin free life on this earth, His crucifixion and death by the hands of those He loved, His walk thru the valley of the shadow of death and His conquering of death in the three days He was descended, the return of a living Messiah to earth for forty days, and His ascension into Heaven and the Throne of His Father, our Creator and Father, Jesus is the only begotten Son of our Father who is in Heaven, and His Kingship while at the right side of His Father in Heaven, His love is continuous and forever, accept Jesus and become a child of God through the debt of payment that Jesus paid for sins He did not commit

Apr 22nd Can you make a plan, yes, rather you complete it is not your decision, if you run into a physical barrier you go over it, around it or even under it, when you run into a spiritual barrier what do you do, someone will escort you through that barrier, what you find on the other side is up to who leads you, if a principalities leads you you have put your destiny in satan's hand, what do you do, you invite the Holy Spirit into your life by accepting a King that resides in Heaven, a King who resides on the right of our Creator and Heavenly Fathers right side, a King and Savior who gave up their life for you, Jesus Christ who paid it all, don't wait on an answer Jesus is the answer, there is no other way Jesus Christ is the Way, have the assurance

Jesus Christ and the Holy Spirit give, know that you are heading for a reunion and not just the valley of death

Apr 23rd As long as we are walking on terra firma everything is ok, we have no worries, but when we begin to sink in the mud we start looking for a way out, you may find solid ground for a moment but it seems we get caught up in the same quagmire again and again there is only one way out, you will never see it if you never see Him, Jesus Christ is the only Path, He is the only Way, the paths of this world always end up at the same place, death, Jesus Christ path is straight and narrow, His path avoids the first death, by avoiding the first death you will not be subject to the second death of judgement, Jesus will say I knew him, not I never knew him, Jesus is the Path, Jesus is the Light, Jesus is the Way, the only Way, everything else is a copy that will fade away, Jesus said He would not forsake you or leave you, Jesus will never fade away and through Him life in abundance is assured

Apr 24th Every day is a day to rejoice with the Lord and in the Lord, to know Jesus Christ as your Lord and Savior is to know assurance, assurance that you will live an eternity in a New Heaven and a New Earth in a New Jerusalem, if you want assurance there is only one place to find it, you can find it in Jesus, no were else is one hundred percent guaranteed, you can search for artifacts of old, they will get you no were, you can have prestige and fame in the life you have here on earth, they will get you nowhere, ask Jesus into your life and grace and mercy will abound, Jesus is the Way period, Jesus is the Truth period, and Jesus is the Life period no one goes to the Father who doesn't go thru the Son, all power was given Jesus Christ because He accomplished the will of the Father, His will was for you to return to Him

Apr 25th Evil people do evil things, they do not know Jesus Christ, and without Jesus we are all subject to this world and the father of lies, Jesus Christ gives us the ability to put on the Armor of God the Armor of God does not only protect us from attacks from the outside, the Armor of God protects us from ourselves, so start with Jesus before you start your day, make Jesus Christ a forethought instead of an afterthought, without Jesus the Armor of God will not even fit, remember to go to the Father you must go through His Son Jesus Christ, to receive what belongs to the Father you must also go through the Son, Jesus Christ is the Way

Apr 26th Let me attempt to explain repentance, repentance does not originate in your mind, repentance does not originate in a heart of stone, repentance originates in a heart of flesh, God said He would replace your heart of stone with a heart of flesh, you cannot transform your real self alone, the only one that can transform you from the inside is someone that knows you from the inside, there is no deceiving of lying about the truth to the Truth, Jesus Christ is the only one that knows you and knows what to change about you, love abounds with Jesus, Jesus has watched you before you were even born, God said He knew you in the womb, He is the only one that has the power to change your heart from stone to flesh, it is not about denial it is about acceptance, accept the gift of life, the total and complete gift of life that Jesus gives you, Jesus said on the cross it is finished, accept Jesus and it will be finished, this world will be washed from your heart and His Kingdom will fill your heart, Jesus will fill your heart with the Holy Spirit, and true repentance begins

Apr 27th You think you have a hard life, if you are still part of this world you do, but there is someone that has had the hardest life, the attempts on His life began from the beginning of this world's existence, His persecution was even more visible after His amazing birth not in a Hospital nor even at Home, His birth was in a manger full of animals, shortly after His birth He was on the run to prevent His murder, He was spit upon, beaten, scourged, and finally crucified by the world for crimes He never committed, He was crucified for sins He never committed, in the end He fought and conquered the world all the way to the Throne room of God, yes He also conquered death, He did this for you and me, He did this because it was the will of His Father, He did this because of love for the Creator and the created, Jesus Christ is our King, Jesus Christ is our Savior

Apr 28th Where can you find everything you need or will ever need, in the hands of Jesus Christ, all of heaven will cry out worthy is the Lamb, this world will be right when all of creation cries out worthy is the Lamb, the word of God says every knee will bow and every tongue confess Jesus Christ is Lord, it is to late then, accept Jesus now, today, your life is but a vapor, please don't put of eternity, the Trinity waits on your decision, Jesus is knocking on the door, accept Him and live with Him forever, deny Him and He will deny you to the only Judge in creation that has the power over eternal death, our Creator, our Father, Jesus's Father the only true God, the God of Abraham And Isaac, creations God

Apr 29th Before Jesus Christ, the Lion from the tribe of Judah, returns, his triumphant victory will be felt, all of creation will herald Him and His sacrifice the Lamb, the rocks will not hold their silence anymore, the Lamb is worthy, sin has been washed away by His blood, the opportunity to unite with Jesus Christ is so important to our Father who is in Heaven, He holds His Son's return, He will delay His return until He knows the last one has accepted His Son Jesus Christ as Savior and King, all that will be saved from the second death will met their triumphant King to reign with Him forever in a new Heaven and a new Earth from a new temple in a new Jerusalem, a temple that holds the actual throne room of God, a throne where the river of life begins

Apr 30th Next time you see Jesus make sure it is permanent, for those that know Him as their Lord and Savior it will be, they will be in His presence forever, for those that don't know Him it is the last time they will ever see Jesus, from that point on they will have known who Jesus is but they had already doubted His grace, they will have already doubted His love, they would have already doubted His identity, they will have already denied Him, Jesus doesn't tell a lie, He said if you deny Him He will deny you to the Father, understand that whatever you believe, or whoever you believe in, there is life eternal, you will spend it in paradise or you will spend it forever banished from the presence of God in a pit that has no bottom, the solution to the lies of this world has been given by the blood of Jesus, accept Him for who He is, the only begotten Son of God

God Made You

May 1st As we see society decay, don't wonder why, our Lords word tells us that this will happen, rejoice, this is a sign of His return, Jesus Christ said He would take care of those of us that belong to Him, the world has many agendas but the Word of God has only one agenda, Salvation, the world will end and all of its agendas will fail, but the word of God will prevail through eternity, I will go to sleep one day because sin brought death but when I awake my King, my Lord and Savior will be there to greet me, He has already paid my price through eternity with Him and Our Father, I have no other judgement awaiting me because I have already been judged and set free, praise His Holy Name, praise the name and Trinity of Jesus Christ

May 2nd It is good with my soul, knowing that Jesus Christ is King of Kings Lord of Lords, it is good with my soul, knowing that Jesus Christ is the only begotten Son of God, it is good with my soul, knowing that Jesus Christ is my Redeemer and Savior, it is good because Jesus paid a price for me that I would never be capable of paying myself, before redemption we were lost and had no chance to return to our Creator, the one and only God, know that this is not your final place of rest, through Jesus we live on in a room in a mansion that Jesus prepared for all those that have accepted the gift of eternal life He gives to us, ask and you will receive, He knows the purpose of our hearts and the truth of our request, know, ask and receive Jesus Christ as Lord and Savior

May 3rd This life is temporary, this means there is something after temporary, if this life is temporary everything in this world is temporary, if you base your life on the solutions of this world you base it on temporary, Jesus told pontius pilate His kingdom was not of this world, obviously Jesus's kingdom is not temporary, satan's ownership of this world is only temporary, Jesus will return to subdue the nations and this world, we will have a one world government and it will be led by Jesus Christ, his kingship is permanent, don't settle for temporary, the permanent answer to everything is Jesus, the only begotten Son of God, to Him all power was given permanently, Jesus is the answer the only answer, stop believing in the mimicry and lies of the devil, believe in the Truth, believe in Jesus Christ

May 4th A little late today but Jesus is always on time, He has the power to endure and support you and me throughout the ages of this world and on into the eternity of the next, all power was given to Him by His Father and our Creator, our God, He is worthy of all worship and prayer, a prayer through Jesus is just the same as a prayer to our Heavenly Father, to worship Jesus Christ is worshipping the Father, Jesus Christ was given the power of Gods strong right Hand and He wields the power of the Father in Truth and in Light, Jesus Christ is both loving and caring to those that have chosen Him in their hearts, yet has the power to stop any adversary, Jesus Christ name invokes His power, Jesus said He would not leave us or forsake us, this is Truth, rely on Him that was slain for you, rely on Him who conquered death, rely on Him that was resurrected and returned to His Father's side in Heaven, you can rely on Jesus

May 5th The Bible speaks about the magnificence of the thrown of God, the Bible also speaks of the strong right

Hand of God, the capabilities of our Creator are limitless, why did He send His only begotten Son to die for you and me, because a price had to be paid, a price that no one else in all of creation could pay, Jesus was the only one that could redeem you, Jesus was the only one that could walk the Redeemers walk, Jesus was the only one worthy, and He did, He paid the price for your sin, the wages of sin is death, Jesus has saved us from the judgement, Jesus has saved us from a second death, Jesus has saved us from the bottomless pit, Jesus has redeemed us , we are the adopted children of God, Jesus is worthy of honor and praise and worship and blessings, Jesus is our Redeemer

May 6th It is all about Jesus, our Creator, our Father in Heaven asked His only begotten Son to die for us, and He did, He has shown us the path back into the Heavenly fold, He has given us the means to do it, and He walked the walk, the exact walk you will one day walk, if you have accepted Jesus Christ as your Lord and Savior, He died just as all of us will do, He walked through the valley and conquered death, we will walk with Him through the valley of the shadow of death, His body was transformed and He was resurrected back to His Father's side, our bodies will be transformed and we will meet Jesus Christ, He has already done it all and He knows the way and He is the Way

May 7th Why do people choose to lose, everything created testifies of a Creator, big bang didn't happen, evolution didn't happen, what happened was God created everything you see including you, but He is a loving God, He will not even force you to love Him, He leaves you with a choice, He sent His only begotten Son to save us from our own sin, He leaves you with a choice, if you do not make it to paradise, God did not make that choice, you did, the only insurance of eternity is Jesus Christ, yet people shun Him and He still loves them, He loves them today just as much as He did when He was crucified on the cross, don't deny Him, find the Truth, Jesus is the Truth

May 8th This world is why you have a heart of stone, the world tells you to walk by a person in need, the world leads you when you don't have any reliance on anything other than this world, this world gives you the capability to deny God our Father who is in Heaven, His only begotten Son Jesus Christ, and the Holy Spirit, there are many things in this world that you cannot see but know that it is there, you know that because one of your senses tell you, can you smell a field of flowers, then you can smell the Creator, can you see a sunrise, then you can see the Creator, can you feel the rain, then you can feel the creator, can you feel love then you can feel Jesus, the world will let you deny the Truth, but the world cannot hide the Truth, Jesus is the Truth, the Way and the Life, don't let the created hide your view of the Creator, there is only one way back, Jesus Christ

May 9th You were given a voice when you were created, Adam walked in the Garden with God, he talked with God in the cool of the evening, and he talked with God until sin came into the relationship, until deception entered the picture, until adam talked with satan, our God is a jealous God, still our Creator has provided us a Way, not several ways but one Way, that is through His only begotten Son Jesus Christ, once again we can talk with God in the cool of the evening, we can talk with God anytime we wish, and guess what He is always waiting on you He will respond, you can hear Him as He talks, expect it, Jesus has accomplished everything for you already, one thing, no one goes to the Father without Jesus, love for you has provided the only Sacrifice all you have to do is accept Jesus

May 10th We have to open our eyes and hearts to Jesus Christ, we need to open our eyes and hearts to our Father who is in Heaven, so many times we say we missed that opportunity, so many times we are afraid, or unsure, why, trust in our Lord Jesus Christ, trust in our Father who is in Heaven, when the scouts went out the majority said no there are giants in the land, we are but ants in their eyes, only two saw the opportunity that God had given them, only two saw the gift of God, only two reported that the land was rich, trust in the Lord, He will not forsake you, He will not leave you, the world will hide the gifts of God, look beyond the smoke screen of the world, look for our Savior not the ones that need to be saved

May 11th Look around before you make a move, consult through prayer through the Son and to the Father, today is your day, tomorrow is not guaranteed and yesterday is gone but not forgotten, to forget yesterday ask Jesus to forgive yesterday, begin life anew through our Savior and Lord Jesus Christ, receive the gifts He has for you and use them to benefit others, but first pray, pray that the Holy Spirit is with you and Jesus is on your mind in everything you do, you can do nothing without Him, serve our risen Lord and Savior, don't serve yourself and don't serve the world, serve Jesus Christ, in serving Jesus Christ you are serving our Father who is in Heaven, who is on the

Throne, serve the King of Kings not a deception, not a lie or the father of lies, serve with the love Jesus has for you, praise God the Father through God the Son,

May 12th Is there an earthly comparison to the love Jesus Christ has for us, is there an earthly comparison to the love our Father in Heaven has for us, the closest would be the love a mother has for her children, just as a mother watches a child leave hoping they would even glance back at her, Jesus waits for you to glance His way, just as a mother has an intimate love for her child waiting for a personal relationship with their child again, Jesus also longs for a personal relationship with you and continuously knocks waiting for an answer, a mother will never give up on her child even though she mourns for their return, Jesus also waits for the acceptance of the gift of life He provides, honor your mother because she provided you with life, Honor Jesus because He gives you life eternal

May 13th Don't search anymore, the fountain of youth has been found, its not a fountain at all it is the only begotten Son of our Father who is in Heaven, Jesus Christ holds the keys to the future, He is the only way, there are instructions written to begin your quest to eternity and it is called the Holy bible, the very words of our Creator, we were not left blind, many people claim that they are interpreters of Gods words, they are mimics, there is only one interpreter and He is the Holy Spirit, the very Spirit of Jesus, you don't have to search for answers that are freely given, accept Jesus Christ and all will be revealed and given to you, through His love all is conquered

May 14th Count your blessings, here they are Jesus Christ, our Father in Heaven, and the Holy Spirit, true blessings only come from the Trinity, things of this world that seem like blessings at first often turn into a curse, know where your blessings come from, by knowing Jesus as your Lord and Savior, He said He would give you green pastures and lay you down by still waters, in other words bless you and your life, a Heavenly posture will reveal blessings in your life that you have not even noticed, there is only one way to have this view of life and that is to have a view of the King of Kings Lord of Lords, His blessings flow freely starting with forgiveness of your sins through payment He paid with His blood, eternal life in Heaven is the first blessing you will receive, after that they flow like the river of life flowing from the Throne of God

May15th God has shown us the way thru examples, Jesus Christ showed us the way thru examples, God gave His only begotten Son as payment for our sins, Jesus is the First fruit of the resurrection, the very same resurrection all of the children of God will have a part in, people complain about giving to God, God doesn't ask you to do anything He has not already done, God gave us His only begotten Son, how precious a gift can never be duplicated, satan will attempt to mimic this very act, do not be deceived, the only way not to be deceived is to have the Holy Spirit for discernment, the only way to have the Holy Spirit is to have already accepted the Way, Jesus Christ said He is the Way, He is the Truth, He is the Life, He said He would never leave you, if Jesus said this it is fact, Jesus is our only Redeemer

God Made You

May 16th If you were going to listen to someone would it be someone that has already accomplished the task before you or someone that is only guessing, Jesus Christ has already accomplished everything He ask of you, anything He ask of you He has already done, Jesus is a King of Kings Lord of Lords that leads by example, don't be so gullible as to listen to someone that has never walked the Way, of someone that lies and says they have been there and know, there is only one Way and that is Jesus Christ, He can guide you, He has been there, He and our Father who art in Heaven has left you a written guide because of love, all is provided, even a Holy Spirit to walk with, yet many don't believe, many taunt someone who talks with our Savior, if you don't know your Savior you wouldn't talk or hear from Him, Jesus is the only Way

May 17th The only protection you have against this invasion is Jesus Christ, the invasion of this world through its ideologies and misrepresentations of God's word is rampant, use the armor God has provided, His written word, the Gospel of His only begotten Son, the Holy Spirit, we don't know when persecution will notice us but it is coming, the father of lies has allies everywhere, lost people that turn a blind eye and a deaf ear to our beautiful Lord and Savior Jesus Christ, they do not know, share the ultimate gift of life, share the only eternal gift that our King Jesus Christ provides, be the disciple that feeds His flock

May 18th Why are people blind to the Truth, the world has denied the Truth, the world deceives and lies about the Truth, to know the Truth you must leave this world, Jesus said that my kingdom is not of this world if it were my servants would fight for me, there is no deceptions or lies in what Jesus said, one day He will return to subdue the nations, He will be victorious, you don't have to wait to His return, accept Jesus now, accept forgiveness now, all is given to you from a loving God, one that longed for your return into His fold, yes, until sin we were part of God's kingdom, we walked with Him we talked with Him, return to Him through the precious blood of His only begotten Son, enjoy the reunion of Life that Jesus Christ provides, He is the Way

May 19th What on earth can get you to Heaven, there will be deceptions portrayed by the father of lies, many will believe, there will be deceptions portrayed by man, they are also lies, Gods word plainly states there is only one Way to the Father and that is through the Son, His Son, His only begotten Son is Jesus Christ, there is no other, Jesus is Truth there is no lie in Him, therefore there is no deception in Him, He will provide you a guide to paradise, a guide to help you navigate this world, He is the Holy Spirit and He will always be with you, Jesus will always be with you, God will always be with you, if Jesus is for you no one above, on or below the earth can prevail against you, through Jesus all is possible and His love for you is number one

May 20th Would you go a day without Jesus, people that don't even believe in Him benefit from His existence, they are loved by Jesus just like those that love Him and know Him as King, Lord, and Savior, they will benefit until the end, we have seen the world running on its own power and God destroyed it with water, we cannot exist without His only begotten Son, but, know that in the end those that deny Him He will deny to the Father, He will say I never knew you, find Jesus Christ while you can, He is knocking, He is waiting, once you find Him you will truly realize how life without Him is a life without fulfillment, Jesus is the Way, the Truth, the Light

May 21st Why do people ask how did I make it through that, it was impossible to survive that crash, oh it was my guardian angel, He carries many names King, Lord Messiah, Savior, Truth, Way, Life, but the very best is Jesus, call on the name of Jesus and He will be seen and felt, tomorrow is not promised, but if you get there get there with Jesus, don't get there without Him, don't go there without Him, someone is on your side, make sure it is the King of Kings Lord of Lords, don't let it be the king of lies, secure tomorrow, there is only one Way, accept our Lord and Savior Jesus Christ today

May 22nd It is easy if you look toward the Throne and not toward the world, you may ask is this all real, is the word of God actually what it says, can anybody love someone that much, especially me, God the Father is real as creation will prove, Jesus is real, to know Him talk with Him, open your Heart and you will see the Holy Spirit, and yes the word of God is all Truth it is His word, the words of Jesus Christ are all True, He is the Way ,the Truth, and the Life, and yes the Holy Spirits words are all also True proven thru His actions, and Their love is real, quit judging yourself, They want you just the way you are, they already know you intimately, They know your problems and They love you, Theirs is a love that last a life time, an eternal lifetime

May 23rd Where do blessings come from, who do you attribute them to, people will say thank God it wasn't worst, but do they really feel in their heart that God intervened, or were they just repeating a phrase with no meaning, yes God intervened, yes Jesus Christ intervened, yes the Holy Spirit intervened, yes the Trinity is something the heart reveals, a heart that has been changed from stone to flesh by the Holy Spirit, blessings only come from God, the world can do nothing because it has no power over the children of God, the devil has no power over those that believe, Jesus told peter that satan wanted to try him but Jesus did not allow it, you are just as important to Jesus as peter was, you will be blessed through Jesus Christ, He will not forsake you

May 24th How do you worship a King who needs nothing, our Creator, our Father who is in Heaven has given all power over to His Son, He gave all power to His only begotten Son because His Son did His Fathers will, He sacrificed Himself for creation, He sacrificed Himself for you and me, He sacrificed Himself for friend and enemy alike, He sacrificed Himself because He loves His Father and He loves you, you no longer have a price to pay, Jesus Christ has paid that price, know that you can return to a Heavenly relationship with God just the way you are, because of Jesus you don't have to stay in a world of immorality, you can enjoy a world full of the love of the Trinity

May 25th God gives us opportunities to see Him every day, sometimes all you have to do is stop and look behind you, you have heard the saying slow down and smell the coffee, well slow down and see Jesus, He is always right there with you, but when He tries to talk with you distractions get in the way, slow down and let your Savior talk with you, slow down and see what He has already done for you, slow down and feel His love for you, it is not Jesus that is running it is you, He has been knocking, stop and open the door of your heart, your heart is where a relationship lives not your mind, you do have a Savior and His name is Jesus Christ, you do have a Lord and He is the only begotten Son of God, Jesus is your King of Kings, Lord of Lords, and He loves you

May 26th God's creation is beautiful and relaxing, had a hard day, stop at the end of it and look at the sunset, look at the stars, relax and watch the squirrels play, humble yourself and know that Jesus Christ is Lord of Lords, that He is your Savior, that He will not Forsake you or leave you, that He will walk with you through the valley of death were ever it may end, that He is our Comforter, that He is the only begotten Son of God, Jesus Christ has an unstoppable love for you, He went through the agonizing death of the cross for you, for He so loved the world that He gave His only begotten Son for it, yes Jesus has scars of love, those scars are for you, to know Him is to love Him

May 27th Why except a maybe, in this world dominated by man you can reach many conclusions, the outcome may not be the same for every time, don't bet your life on that, Jesus stated to the sanhedrin at twelve years old that He was doing His Fathers business, Jesus Christ came to fulfill His Fathers will, and His Fathers will was for His Son to pay a price for us, what He paid for was our sin, He had none, how He paid for it was by losing His own life so we could live, His outcome will never change, Jesus fulfilled His Fathers will out of love for us the first time, He conquered death for us, He paid that price in full for those that except Him, for those that except the Truth, your death at the final Judgement assures one thing, the bottomless pit, accept Jesus Christ and live, He is the only Way

May 28th Reading the word of God is a good thing, but it won't get you to Heaven, it can only lead you to Heaven, the whole bible is needed to understand, to understand the who of the bible, the who is Jesus Christ, the Cornerstone, the Key to fully understanding the word of God, Jesus provides a mentor in your life, that person is the Holy Spirit, the very Spirit of God, the Holy Spirit will inspire you to move closer to Jesus the Son, through Jesus the Son you will come closer to God the Father, without the Cornerstone you are not complete, you will never leave this world, you will always be a part of this world, with Jesus Christ you live in this world but you are not part of this world, and when this world is replaced by a new Earth you will continue till eternity is complete

May 29th The world is not the only problem, those that don't know choose not to know, those that don't see choose not to see, those that don't feel choose not to feel, those that don't taste choose not to taste, if a heart remains stone that person has made that choice, why did God let this or that happen, He didn't you did, in the Garden the earth was given to us, when we left the Garden everything was lost to us, God has given man a Way back, God so loved the world that He gave his only begotten Son, God sacrificed his Son to reclaim His creation, you are His creation, God loves you, Jesus has paid the price for you to return, open the door to your heart and all your senses will follow

May 30th Why should you pray, because you can't do it on your own, the word of the Lord says for we wrestle not against flesh and blood, share the Gospel of Jesus Christ and pray, the bible says that our fight is against principalities, against powers, against the rulers of the darkness of this world, against spiritual wickedness in high places, pray continuously, for those that believe, the bible says the Angel of the Lord encampeth round about them that fear Him, and delivereth them, you are not alone, put on the full Armor of God and put your full faith in Jesus Christ

May 31st Someday our King will wholly return, our King, Jesus Christ, the only begotten Son of God, did not leave us entirely, He left us with a comforter, the Holy Spirit abides in those that have accepted Jesus as their Lord and Savior, Jesus said He would not leave us nor forsake us, Jesus hears your prayers, His Spirit hears and prays for us when we are not capable, prayer is answered, open your eyes, open your heart, don't let the world deceive you anymore, pray for the scales of this world to fall from your eyes, every knee shall bow, every tongue will confess, above earth, on earth, and below earth, every knee, every tongue, Jesus Christ is Lord

June 1st You believe in what you can see, do you believe in what you can't see, have you ever received something you needed in your life and wonder where did that come from, I really needed that, that was a life saver, do you know a blessing when you receive it, praise the name of your Lord and Savior Jesus Christ, He will provide, His provisions come when they are needed, His comfort and love is everlasting, you can see creation bless the Creators, bless the Trinity, bless the Father, Son, and Holy Spirit, this is where your power lives, the world only mimics the Truth, the world is not the Creator but the created, rely on Jesus, He is intercessor, He is the Way

June 2nd Feeling alone, look toward Jesus, He knows the feeling, He has walked the walk, when He died He was alone, but the Good news, Jesus conquered death, He is alive, feeling alone, look toward Jesus the only begotten Son of God, He said He would not forsake you or leave you, praise the Father, He has given us a dedicated Savior, Jesus deserves the title King of Kings, Lord of Lords, all power has been given to Jesus Christ, oh what a friend we have in Jesus, if you don't know Jesus Christ, get to know Him, He knows you and He wants you just the way you are

June 3rd There is only one interpreter of the word of God, He is the Holy Spirit, one man cannot interpret alone, the revelations which are in the word of God are only revealed by the Spirit of Jesus Christ, to fully know the words of the Father you must know the Son, Jesus Christ is the key to the kingdom of God, He is the key to eternity, He is the key to everything, without Him there is no communication with the Father, literal, yes, Truth, yes, everything that is written by our Father who is in Heaven can only be understood through the acceptance and belief in Jesus, when it comes to the understanding of the word of God, depend on His only begotten Son Jesus Christ, without Him a sentence cannot be formed

June 4th Jesus cries when you cry, Jesus laughs out loud when you laugh out loud, Jesus knows all your emotions and He shares them with you, you cannot have a closer friend, you cannot have a more caring friend, you cannot have a more loving friend, but, Jesus Christ will not come into your life uninvited, enhance your life, open the door and let Jesus in, He shares the emotions of your heart, and cares about the outcome of your life, it is True, oh what a friend we have in Jesus, Jesus said He would not forsake you or leave you, through Jesus all is forgiven, Salvation is free to those that receive and believe in Jesus

June 5th You were created for a purpose, that purpose was distorted by satan in the garden of eden, so many believe the lie that the father of lies has perpetrated since the fall, you are not worthy, God doesn't care, you have no purpose, all lies, God so loved the world that He gave His only begotten Son, this is the Truth, Jesus Christ did the will of His Father when He sacrificed His life for you and me, don't let the sacrifice of Jesus Christ pass by you without accepting the only Way back to the reality of why you were created, don't accept the lies that bombard you daily from the devil, the Truth is God loves you, the Truth is Jesus loves you, the Truth is they long for you to return and have given a Way for you to come home

June 6th If the world couldn't hold the volumes of books about everything Jesus Christ did while alive here on earth to include all the miracles He did, what is the problem, people don't believe because they can't see, do you believe Jesus Christ is alive today, do you believe Jesus died on a cross thru crucifixion for your sins, do you believe He conquered death, that He was resurrected and sits on the right hand of the Fathers throne in Heaven, let me tell you Jesus is still in the miracle business, but why, why because it is the Fathers will, He knows every hair on your head, He knows when it is time to come Home, if man would let Jesus do His business all the miracles He still does could be clearly seen, open your heart and eyes to the Son of God

June 7th How does man know when the moon will be full, because there is a cycle, a design, an intelligent design, all you see , all you will ever see was created by the Trinity, everything created was created for a purpose, creation includes you, we were created in God's image to tend to His creation, we were created to fellowship with God, to walk in the cool of the evening with Him, don't let creation cloud your vision from the Creator, that which was created is not the creator of anything, we have a sovereign Lord, He is the Alpha and Omega, that includes everything in between, there is a purpose for your life, walk with God in the cool of the evening, walk with God in the cool of the morning, walk with God always

June 8th God has given us everything we need to return home, the map has been drawn by His only begotten Son, He is the Way the only Way, people have been deceived by other people into believing there are other ways, and people choose to believe this great lie perpetrated by the father of lies, Find the Way thru the written words of the Father who is in heaven, when you find the Son you will again find our Heavenly Father, you will be given a teacher thru the Son, that Teacher is the Holy Spirit, don't rely on man to get you out of the miss we are in, rely on the very Son of our Creator Jesus Christ, When you find Him your search is over, all will be given to you, thru love

June 9th Is there something political about religion, yes, that is why you don't hear religion criticized in politics, is there something political about a relationship, yes, that's why Christianity is criticized in politics, man's religions are just that, they do not interfere with man's politics, a Christians relationship with their King, Jesus Christ, is a different story, the love of Jesus Christ gets in the way of man, the love of Jesus Christ has only one agenda, the will of the Father, the will of the Father is to restore the relationship with you, the relationship you were created for in the beginning, the relationship we had with our Creator before sin, the closeness we lost, restoration , rejuvenation, love, Jesus Christ

June 10th Jesus will not fail you, Jesus did not fail His Father, Jesus does not fail, He is the Way, He is the Truth, He is the Life, no one goes to the Father except thru the Son, man will claim and claim and claim there is another way, man will throw abomination after abomination at the children of God, hold fast to Jesus, He said things will get worse, but praise God things will get better, Jesus Christ will return and Jesus Christ will prevail over man and satan, all power is given to Him thru His Father and Creator of all

June 11th Everyone thinks they know a better way, everyone wants to add to or subtract from, oh it doesn't really mean that, sounds like satan in the garden, did He really say that, the words of our Creator are clear, you must read His words first, don't let someone else read and interpret, you read and interpret through the Holy Spirit which is a benefit of Jesus Christ, He said I must go so the Comforter can come, there are many ways to add to or take away from, the word of our Lord says any man or angel who adds to or takes away from Gods word will be accursed, Jesus on the cross said it is finished, there is no second volume, the words of the Trinity are complete and true, start with Jesus if you want clarity, He will not forsake you

June 12th By default you have a spiritual father, through the fault of sin your father has a name, that name is the father of lies, sin brought us into the world of satan, there is a Way back to our origins, there is a Way back to our Father who is in Heaven, that Way has a name , a name above all names, Jesus Christ the only begotten Son of God our Creator, He and He alone is capable of returning you to our original purpose, fellowship with our True Father, the Father of everything, the only living God, our God, do not follow any other name but Jesus Christ, return to your True family the Family of God

June 13th Did you make plans today, if you did who was included in the plan making, if you make the plans alone you only have yourself to blame for those plans, if you make plans with your worldly friends you only have the world to blame, if you make your plans according to the word of God your plans will always succeed, if you make your plans with the Creator instead of the created you will succeed, if you make your plans with Jesus your plans will succeed, make your plans full proof with the Trinity, don't let it be foolish with the world, follow the advice of the one who knows all, Jesus Christ, instead of the world that knows nothing

June 14th Did you make plans today, if you did who was included in the plan making, if you make the plans alone you only have yourself to blame for those plans, if you make plans with your worldly friends you only have the world to blame, if you make your plans according to the word of God your plans will always succeed, if you make your plans with the Creator instead of the created you will succeed, if you make your plans with Jesus your plans will succeed, make your plans full proof with the Trinity, don't let it be foolish with the world, follow the advice of the one who knows all, Jesus Christ, instead of the world that knows nothing

June 15th Accept Jesus Christ as your Lord and Savior, after that you can claim the victory that is associated with the Kingdom of God, after that you can go to the very Throne room of God, you can't claim victory if you have not accepted victory, no one goes to the Father except through the Son, Jesus Christ is the only begotten Son of God, He is the Way, He is the Cornerstone, He is the Key, go to Jesus just the way you are, His blood does the cleansing, His blood makes you acceptable, His blood changes you, you can do nothing without first accepting Jesus, don't ask why if you have not, a little leaven affects all it touches, love Jesus as He loves you, love your neighbor as Jesus loves you, Jesus is the Way, the Truth, and the Life, no one goes to the Father except through Him

June 16th Everyone has an agenda, sure they will help you if you support their cause, that is everyone has an agenda but Jesus Christ, if He had an agenda it would be called Salvation, Salvation for you, yes He died for you, He died through an agonizing death called crucifixion, so Jesus does have an agenda, to save you from an agonizing death that delivers you to a bottomless pit for eternity, This Salvation is given to you just the way you are, so as your heart of stone dissolves into a heart of flesh, a heart that can love as Jesus Christ loves you consider that all Jesus did , He did for you and His Father who also loves you

June 17th If you know who Jesus Christ is, spread His name, if you know what Jesus did spread His Gospel, so many people don't know the Truth, so many people only know the name of Jesus and not the why of the only begotten Son of God, to know Him is to love Him, and to love Him is to share His Gospel, His Gospel was never meant to stop, His Gospel is meant to be told and retold, no one will be left blind, every knee shall bow every tongue will confess Jesus Christ is Lord, don't wait to confess, confess now, know Him now, Jesus was God yesterday, He is god today, and He will be God tomorrow, He is the Alpha and Omega

June 18th You cannot do it on your own, you cannot survive this world alone, you cannot survive eternity alone, believe in the only Way, believe in the Truth, believe in the Life, believe in Jesus Christ, the Good Shepard, with Him all is possible, without Him nothing is possible, you can search and search and search and never secure a spot in Heaven on your own, quit searching and open the door, give an invitation to your King, to your Lord, answer His call, with Him all things are possible, with Him eternity is obtainable, with Him your life is changed to one of love not hate, praise Jesus Christ holy name

June 19th Stop and spend time with Jesus Christ this morning, He accomplished salvation for all, to claim eternity with Him accept and know Him, it is free for the asking, why is it free because God so loved the world that He gave His only begotten Son for it, we are captives, Jesus has set the captives free, you are free He has opened the prison doors, walk thru them into the arms of Jesus, don't choose a life behind the false hood of satan, open your eyes to the Truth, open your eyes to Jesus

June20th Jesus is Lord, why do so many deny who He is, you can live hear on earth and enjoy all the delights it has to offer, you can say I am ok, I am free, without Jesus you will never be free, He came to set the captives free, your life here on earth is not the beginning and the end, you will never die, the problem is where will you spend eternity, the solution is Jesus Christ, He is the Alpha, your Alpha, He is the Omega , your Omega, accept the price that Jesus Christ paid for you, spend eternity with your Creator or spend eternity without Him, you have a God and Judgement has already been made, Jesus is the Way

June 21st On father's day lets honor our Heavenly Father, how can we do this, by honoring His only begotten Son, so many people don't know of His Son or why Jesus Christ is, He is because He was the only one capable of accomplishing what was needed to return us to the Fold of Heaven, He is the Good Shepard, He was crucified for our sine, He did conquer death, He was resurrected back to the right of our Father who is in Heaven, Jesus was given all power, to honor the Son is to Honor the Father, so if you want to honor God today honor His Son today, honor Jesus Christ, don't let the sacrifice of our Heavenly Father go unrecognized today, don't let the sacrifice of His Son go unclaimed today

June 22nd To gain victory in our life's here on earth we must look toward Jesus, to gain victory after this life we must look toward Jesus, Jesus takes nothing away, He only gives, satan would have you believe that all is taken from you if you seek Jesus, all will be taken away from satan in the end including his freedom to corrupt, satan only deceives and mimics the works of Heaven, in the end all will fall apart for Him, and all will fall apart for those that have not accepted our King and Savior Jesus Christ, everyone will know the solution, everyone will not choose the solution, Jesus Christ is the solution, Jesus Christ is the only solution

June 23rd There is a right Way, and there is a wrong way, there are thousands of wrong ways, there is only one right Way, that right Way is Jesus Christ, no other explanations are needed, nothing needs to be added or taken from, His Way is the perfect Way, the only begotten Sons Way is the Fathers Way, it is given to us freely, Jesus has accomplished all, on the cross Jesus said it is finished, and so it is, the only additions or subtractions come from two sources, an unsaved man and satan to deceive us, one out of ignorance and one that knows the Truth but will never attain it, both lost, there is not another chance for satan, there is for man, accept Jesus Christ as your Savior and return to our Father who is Creator of all

June 24th The principalities are hard at work against the Kingdom of God, against the Kingdom of Jesus Christ, against those that have accepted Jesus Christ as Lord and Savior, for those that do not know the Truth the agents of satan have no work at all, non-believers of Jesus are exactly where they want them, this life is short, but it is all the time you have to make a decision that will last into eternity, find the Truth, the Way, and the Life while you can, find Jesus and accept Him as King, this life her in this world is all the time you have, know the Truth

June 25th Come into the fold of Jesus Christ, He is the Good Shepard, He will never leave you or forsake you, don't settle for a temporary solution, ask and you shall receive a permanent solution, Jesus Christ will always be available for you, you are the lost sheep He is looking for, you are the sheep He will recover on the Sabbath, you are the sheep He will stop and secure before continuing, you are important to Jesus, you alone can call His name and He will answer, this commitment to you is all because of love, an undying love for you that only you can satisfy, Jesus loves all of us and has proven that love through the cross and beyond death, you are loved

June 26th What are people looking for, they feel as though they have to be part of the answer, that somehow they have to contribute to the solution, well here is the answer, His name is Jesus Christ, He is the solution to all your problems, He alone is the only solution that you will ever need, if you have to be part of the answer you are, here is our part sin, but praise God that thru the cleansing blood of Jesus Christ sin is no longer part of the equation, when you repent and turn to our Lord and Savior, our Redeemer, our

King, sin is forgotten it id as far away as the east is from the west, Jesus makes us whole, Jesus makes us part of the Family of God again

June 27th We all have a decision to make, life is full of joys, but the ultimate joy you can find is not in the bottom of a bottle, the ultimate joy you can subject yourself to is when you accept your Lord and Savior Jesus Christ as Lord, joy will fill your glass daily from the word of God then, understanding will come through the Holy Spirit, fulfillment will happen at the reunion of life with our Creator, accept Jesus today, tomorrow may be too late

June 28th The Word of the Lord is a standalone revelation, the input for the bible only had one author, and there is only one Truth, when we study The Word of God look for the guidance of the Holy Spirit, he has no bias, we are often influenced in our understanding of His Word by our cultures, our cultures have no place in the understanding, our relationships, only one relationship matters and that is your relationship with Jesus Christ, the world has nothing to add or subtract, peer pressure has nothing to add or subtract, understand the Word of God thru the One who wrote it, not the ones that read it

June 29th When you run a race you run to win it, when you run that race and win it you wait for another race, everyone starts the race even, but it is always the same here in the world, you win a race only to start again, there is one race in life you can win and never have to race again, that is the run to eternity, it can be won permanently through Jesus Christ, He has run that race and won it once and for all, Jesus said we can be joint winners through His victory, all we have to do is claim it, claim victory through Jesus Christ, oh what a friend we have in Jesus, Jesus said no better friend can you have than one that will lay down His life for you, Jesus did, claim victory through Jesus

June 30th No matter what you are about to do pray, no matter where you are going pray, pray for those that don't know to pray, pray, pray, pray, Jesus will be with you always, say his name when you pray, say in the name of Jesus Christ, know that He carries your prayer to our loving Father who art in Heaven, know the power in His name , every knee shall bow, every tongue confess, the demons know Him and fear Him, so many men are blind to the Truth, know Jesus Christ, you will be set free

July 1st Jesus is there even when unplanned events happen, He is always available for you, all we really need to know is the Word, the Word will set you free, not the world but the Word, follow Jesus's example to live a joyful life, His is the only way to salvation, be prepared at all times to help each other, Jesus is always available to you, always be available to each other, yes, let people see Jesus in you, He said He would never forsake you or leave you, His example to us is how we need to walk our lives, the volumes could not hold all the things He did, start filling your own volumes in the name of Jesus

July 2nd The cost for one sin is the same cost for ten thousand sins, a second death, we are not capable of paying the price of even one sin, we are lost, God not only provides a way out of temptations He also provided a Way to pay for sin, all sin, He sacrificed His only begotten Son for a world that did not care, His love for us is why He asked this of His Son and His Son said not My will be done but Your will be done, Jesus Christ had no sin, He took on the sins of the world to set us free from the a second death, a death that would separate us from God forever, Jesus made the payment, accept Jesus Christ and you will be free from the world and reunited with a loving Creator that gave you a choice

July 3rd Jesus deserves the praises, Jesus deserves the love, He has provided for us a Way home instead of the one way ticket to hell we deserve, Jesus took our sins from us, past present and future sins, Jesus took them all to the grave with Him and returned triumphant over the devil and death, He has returned to His Father's side and is an advocate for those that chose Him over death, He is King of Kings Lord of Lords, He is deserving of all our worship, because of Jesus we can say we live

July 4th Almost time for fireworks, make everyday a day of celebration, you can do that through Jesus Christ, He will share revelations of the Kingdom of God every day, as you look, as you study, Jesus will awaken you to His love and the love of the Father, the world has nothing worthwhile to offer if it does not come from the King of Kings, all good things come from the Lord of Lords, He does not bring evil, evil is a gift of this world, it has nothing good to give, if you are not a part of the Kingdom of God you are a part of the world, through Jesus we will give good things, we will love our neighbors, we will rejoice in Jesus, we will be guided by His Spirit, the three, the Father, the Son, and the Holy Spirit are in agreement, join the Trinity, accept Jesus Christ and repent

July 5th Worship our only God and His only begotten Son Jesus Christ today, you don't have to be in a certain building, you can worship Jesus Christ were you are, stop what you are doing and give Him a minute of your time, dedicate this time to Him, after all He dedicated His whole life, He dedicated eternity to you, dedicate your life to Him, praise Jesus Christ, lay claim to what Jesus has given you, become washed in the blood of the lamb today, right now, tomorrow is not guaranteed

July 6th Once you have accepted Jesus Christ what happens to you, your sins are forgiven, you are given a counselor and teacher thru the Holy Spirit, you begin to see the world for what it is, not what was created in the beginning but what the created has made it, your heart will begin to soften from a heart of stone to a heart of flesh, you will start to see things in a different Light, a light that shows the reality of man and how and why he is lost without Jesus Christ, Jesus is the Key to the prison, He is the Cornerstone, He is the only Way, He is the Cure for all that is wrong, accept Jesus Christ today and today the scales will fall from your eyes

July 7th Remember one thing, you are never alone, when all your friends have left you, when your family ignores you, when you are the lowest of low, there is still a friend that is with you, Jesus Christ said there is no better a friend than one that will lay down his life for you, your friend Jesus Christ did exactly that, He died for you so you would not have to die a second death, oh what a friend we have in Jesus, praise His holy name Praise the only begotten Son of God, rely on Jesus He is refreshing, He is renewing, He is King of Kings Lord of Lords, He is my Savior, He is your Savior, He is deserving of all praise

July 8th Jesus Christ is not about everything you want, He is about everything you need, everything you want is not always good for your life or the relationship you have found with the King of Kings Lord of Lords, Jesus provides all your needs all the time, and more, an abundance and more, His love for you is never ending, reach out and touch your Saviors hand today, right now, know that thru Jesus you have secured your future in paradise, Jesus Christ is the best friend you will ever have, His love for you is undying, what He wants to give you is life, and in abundance

July 9th Whatever you are doing stop when and say hello or may God bless you today, acknowledge people, all you have to do is follow Jesus Christ example, love one another as you love yourself, Jesus died on the cross acknowledging everyone, His gift is free for everybody, so acknowledge people, sometimes we need a boost, someone saying hello may just be what brightens our day, follow the example that our King has shown us, He is our Savior, plant a seed, eventually that seed may become a tree, let Jesus Christ be your fertilizer for life, He controls the fruit of the tree of Life

July 10th What takes precedence in your life, is yourself, is it your family, is it your country, what should take precedence is your Lord and Savior Jesus Christ, start with Him and He will fulfill the rest, He will never forsake you or leave you, it is better to have a Risen Savior and King of Kings on your side than not to have Him, He longs to comfort you, He even said I must leave so I can send the Comforter, the Holy Spirit, a piece of our loving God to lead and guide you thru this life onto eternity

July 11th So many people say prove that Jesus is real, prove that God is real, look in the mirror and prove They are not real, the reality of a Creator is creation, one beetle does not exist there are thousands of different beetles, one ant does not exist there are thousands of different ants, one bird does not exist there are thousands of different birds, however, there is only one Way, one Way to continue life, life with our Creator, our God, our Savior, that Way is Jesus Christ, to continue life in a new body that ascends you to meet Jesus Christ and continue life with the Father and the Son, or, a new body to meet your Savior to have Him tell you I never knew you and be judged to descend into the bottomless pit where you will know the Truth and never will see the Truth again

July 12th Go to a reunion today, a reunion with all your sisters and brothers in Christ Jesus, revive your relationship with the One that shed His blood for you, the One who descended and continued to conquer death for you the One that ascended and carries all your prayers to a loving Father and Provider, this is all possible because of Jesus, He said not my will but your will when His Father asked, you are alive because He lives

July 13th When did we forget we were created by a loving Father, after the fall, how long after the fall, God has sent us reminders of who He is, He has sent us prophets, He has used signs such as the rainbow to remind us of who He is, ultimately He sent His only begotten Son, when the end comes it is going to be hard to say I didn't know, learn His final message of Love, accept His final message of Love, accept Jesus Christ, accept God's last messenger Jesus Christ as your Savior and Lord, become a child of the one true living God again, there is only one Way Jesus Christ, He is the key to returning to where we belong, we belong in the garden looking out not outside looking in, one Way Jesus Christ

July 14th Pray today, pray right now, it is not about God it is about you, one prayer is not from the heart, if you are so mournful that you only say one word in a prayer it is known from our Father in Heaven, it is known by His only begotten Son Jesus Christ, it is completed by the Holy Spirit, your cries are heard and acted upon, and when you can't pray the Holy Spirit will pray for you, you are never forsaken you, our Heavenly Father loves us Jesus Christ loves us, the Holy Spirit loves us, they all know when your heart is broken and care

July 15th Today is your day stop giving into the world, give in to the majesty of our King Jesus Christ, He is the Way, the only Way, He has been waiting on you since eternity began, He wants to insure that through all of His sacrifices that we see eternity together, that we drink from the river of Life that flows from the Throne of God in the New Jerusalem which Has the Tree of Life on both sides that we can freely eat from, Jesus Christ has provided all these things for us, His Father told Him of His will and He said not my will but your will be done, we are alive for a reason, start serving our one and only Savior Jesus Christ

God Made You

July 16th When right is wrong and wrong is right, look around you, it is being promoted every day, signs are everywhere yet we choose to turn a blind eye to it , it will be too late for redemption when you die, the time to choose Jesus Christ is now, the time to accept Him as your Lord and Savior is today, tomorrow may never come, Jesus is waiting on you and has been since the day you were born, He will wait, but why, give your life over to Jesus Christ, insure your salvation is complete, do it this morning pray to Jesus, ask Him to come into your life, be saved today, I accept Jesus Christ as my Lord and Savior today

July 17th Jesus is the reason, Jesus Christ is the reason for everything, His accomplishments here on earth were for you and they were because of His Fathers will, everything Jesus did was out of pure love for you and our Creator, our Father, who art in Heaven hallowed be they name, Thy kingdom come , Thy will be done, praise Jesus, praise God, their love overcame us, Jesus is the only reason we can return home , now we have another destiny, that destination is Heaven and not the bottomless pit, Jesus provided us this option, accept Jesus Christ and return hometo paradise

July 18th Pray today, Jesus is listening, pray today not for yourself but for others, leave your prayers today so that others can pray for your needs, pray today so others can petition our King of Kings, He will answer, He wants to hear our voices, unity in prayer is just that, fellowship with others, fellowship with our Lord of Lords, make Jesus number one in your prayer chain, let us all pray, pray for the needs of others today, of each other's today, Jesus is reliable and He wants you to rely on Him, no one goes to the Father bur thru the son, Jesus is the last link in your prayer chain and He is the strongest link, pray today, pray in Jesus Christ

July 19th All we need to do is open our hearts instead of our minds, your mind will deceive you, your heart will never deceive you, that's why God said I will give you a heart of flesh instead of stone, the accuser will deceive your mind with illusions and mimicry's, your heart knows the Truth and the Truth will set you free, Jesus Christ is the Truth, Jesus Christ has already paid the way, He has set the captives free, He is the Key, He is the Cornerstone, you can rely on Him, He will rebuke the storm, ask and you shall receive, call on the name of Jesus

July 20th There is really no reason to be lost anymore, un less of course you never knew, tell them about your Jesus, tell the about my Jesus, Jesus said that there is only one way back to our Father and that is through Him, if you know Him you know the Truth, if you don't know Him you are searching for the Truth, if you deny Him there is no Truth in you and your destiny is with the father of lies, share the Gospel today, share the story of Jesus Christ today, lead someone to Salvation today

July 21st Jesus hasn't gone anywhere, He still responds to our needs out of love that is deeper than any worldly love, He knocks continuously because of this love, if this is an annoyance to you, you need to wake up, recognize that you are lost to this world, so many support the world having no idea who created the world, they worship the created not the creator, they do not know the Creator, they do not know the Father, Son, or Holy Spirit, yet they want to tell you how to live, share the wonderful Gospel of Jesus Christ, that is our commission, let the lost know, the decision is theirs, plant a seed for Jesus today

July 22nd If you are lost, there is hope, if you have made a mistake, there is a solution, anything you do, there is a solution, Jesus Christ is the answer to all three, Jesus is the Way, the only Way, He can help, He wants to help, ask and you will receive, first ask Jesus to become your Shepard, then, His reward, becomes your reward, Jesus is the Way, Truth, and Life, no one goes to the Father without first receiving the Son, accept Jesus Christ as Lord and Savior, become a joint air with Jesus, through Jesus, His love will set you free

July 23rd Every day, every minute of the day, Jesus Christ is watching you, not to see what you are doing and accusing you, watching and waiting for you to turn around and turn to Him, He is waiting to help you, to lead you to green pastures, to lay you down by still waters, to lead you to paradise, the accuser is also watching you waiting for an accusation to carry to the throne, the devil carries his accusations to the throne, the throne that is occupied by the Father and the Son, Jesus Christ dismisses him with this, I have already paid the price for this child of God, Jesus Christ has this authority because He did the Fathers will, to know the Fathers will you must know the Father, to know the Father you must know the Son, accept Jesus Christ today and the Truth will set you free

July 24th Did you miss Jesus today, He misses you, He is always watching and waiting for you, He is in a place of authority to support you, why, because He loves you and He did lay His life down for you, when you decide He is waiting , if you have already accepted Jesus as your personal Savior and Lord then pray to our Advocate on the Throne, pray to the King of Kings that did shed His blood for you, for your life, for your Salvation, Jesus Christ is Lord and Savior to all who accept His gift of life, if you don't know pray to Him now, and yes you will hear His voice

July 25th What is the purpose of your life, is it to serve yourself, is it to perpetuate yourself, no it is not about you at all, the purpose of your life is to perpetuate the Kingdom of God, the purpose of your life is to serve God our Father, to fellowship with our Creator, the purpose of your life is to serve a Risen Savior, no better love does a man have, Jesus gave up His life, spread the Gospel, spread the good news of salvation, serve each other, love your neighbor as you love yourself

July 26th Life is not meant to be a guessing game, it is not meant to be a how I feel day, or an oh well day, this is what our accuser wants us to believe, we have guidance in the Words of the Lord, the problem is that most people don't know the Words of the Lord, there is only one Bible and there is only one Savior, you need them both, but I don't know where to start, start by accepting Jesus Christ and the rest will be given to you, Jesus Christ is called the Good Shepard, follow His lead and He will lead you to eternity, an eternity of love, an eternity in paradise with our very Creator, our Father who art in Heaven

July 27th Before you delve into life and what it has to offer understand that there are two reality's, before the sin of disobedience to God and after, you can be your own person and you will die your own person, become a child of God again, you cannot do it alone as the world would have you believe, you must have Jesus Christ in your life, you must accept Jesus as your Lord And Savior, after this life there are two reality's Heaven and the bottomless pit, Jesus the only begotten Son of God is the Way the only Way the door is narrow, follow Jesus

July 28th What do you plan to do today, more specifically do you have any plans to grow the Kingdom of God, this is the great commission to share the Good News to share the Gospel of Jesus Christ, know who Jesus Christ is, know what He has done and who He did it for, and why He did it, share the Truth and the Truth will set you free, all you are doing is planting a seed, you may nurture it or you may not, but be assured in this, all glory and praise goes to the Father through the Son, tell someone the story of Jesus today, share the Truth

July 29th What do you have to lose, just your rightful place in eternity, insure you have a seat at the marriage supper of the lamb, start preparing now, the invitation has already been given, accept Jesus Christ as Savior and King, He is the reason, the only reason you are invited, tomorrow the Master may close the door, once the door is closed it will not be opened again, today is the time, right now is the time to accept Jesus, don't wait until it is too late, today you have an advocate in the very Throne room of God, tomorrow the door may be closed, it is not our Fathers wish that anyone is lost, don't wait the opportunity is now to obtain Salvation through our Lord Jesus Christ, grasp His hand

July 30th Where are your thoughts today, have you shared the Gospel of Jesus Christ, our Father who is in Heaven provides chances to intervene in lost people's lives every day, don't miss the opportunity to talk about our one true Savior and Lord Jesus Christ, the adversary is selling a false savior, how is a lost person to know the Truth, we are to share the Truth, the devil is busy at all times trying to sale his messiah, and unfortunately people are buying a false truth, share the real Son of God, share Jesus Christ today, let people see Jesus in you

July 31st You only have one opportunity to accept Jesus Christ, tomorrow is not guaranteed, your life may be taken tonight, you have no idea when your life will end, Jesus Christ knew and He did the Fathers will, you are saved, the price has been paid, you have won through the actions of one, the only begotten Son of God, so many walk around with scales on their eyes, remove the plank, accept Jesus as your Savior and King, do it now, do it today, He is the Good Shepard, He will lead you to Eternity in Paradise

Aug 1st Devote yourself to Jesus Christ, He is already devoted to you, know that you are a sinner and need a Savior, that Savior is Jesus Christ, Know that someone had to die to pay for those sins, Jesus did, know that someone descended to a spiritual battle, which was fought to free you from death, Jesus did the fighting for you, Jesus was victorious over death, Know that Jesus set the captives free and then ascended back to Heaven to sit on the right of our Father who is in Heaven to intercede for you and me, know this Truth and you to will be forgiven and set free

Aug 2nd What do you know this morning, do you know if you serve a risen Savior today, or , do you just think you do, let Jesus in to your heart, you need to allow Him in to your heart fully, not just when you need Him, if you are doing things that you would rather Jesus not see, or maybe you do these things saying to yourself you will be forgiven, Let Jesus in one hundred percent, one hundred percent with Jesus guarantees one hundred percent paradise for eternity, Jesus Christ said if you are lukewarm He will spit you out, He said He would rather you be hot or cold, don't straddle the fence, be one hundred percent for Jesus

Aug 3rd What is it that you think makes you incomplete, a spouse, a child, a home, all good things but they will not complete you, a relationship with your King and Savior will complete you, as a relationship with Jesus Christ grows your completeness will grow with Him, you will realize the Truth and the Truth will set you free, you will find that Jesus Christ is the Way, that he is the Truth, that He is the Life, Jesus has already conquered all the obstacles that were once in the way of Paradise and He gives that key to you freely, accept Jesus and Life will abound

Aug 4th Is it that we lose interest so quickly, satan would have you believe the grass is greener on the other side, we forget that the Creator of the grass paints the grass, Jesus said He would lead you to green pastures, so who gives the greenest pasture, don't let the master of lies deceive you anymore, all satan can do is mimic and then halfheartedly because he knows how easy it is to deceive, put on the whole Armor of God, trust in your Living Risen Savior and He will insure your steps lead you through the narrow door to Paradise, Jesus is the Way, the only Way, don't be deceived anymore

Aug 5th What do you think you can accomplish without Jesus Christ, temporary satisfaction at best, remember, this part of your life is really the smallest part of your life, eternity is a much larger part, and eternity without Jesus Christ is misery and isolation in a pit of despair, know today that your future is secure in Jesus Christ, know that He is the Way, the Truth, and the Life, if you don't know Jesus, learn who He is, talk with Him, He will send a Comforter in the form of the Holy Spirit and revive you and your life, it is not possible to do this alone, pray to Jesus and know Him as your Lord and Savior

Aug 6th We are to serve each other, just as Jesus Christ gave us the example when He walked this earth in the flesh, Jesus still serves us in Heaven, no one goes to the Father except thru the Son, Jesus serves us with the Holy Spirit, His love is never ending, onto death and risen again to sit at the right of our Father in Heaven, look to the example giver, look to the One that gave up His life for a friend, look to Jesus Christ in all things and in all things you will be rewarded even into eternity

Aug 7th Sometimes we are late for important events, mark your calendars today, pray for forgiveness today, pray with a repenting heart, believe in the only Savior given, Jesus Christ, acknowledge that salvation can only be accomplished through Him and in Him, Jesus has already given all, we can do nothing, trust in the One that is trust worthy, Jesus is the final answer, the Son was sent by the Father to redeem all of us, believe and live, Jesus is the reason, the only reason

Aug 8th If you don't have time, well you better make time, eternity is all that lies ahead, Jesus Christ has already paid for your ticket, and by the way He is the only one that can, you do have a couple of choices, and yes they are yours alone, your friends can't help, your family can't help, you must decide, are you going to serve a Ascended Savior, a Savior who sits on the right hand side of our Father who is in Heaven, or, are you going to serve a fallen world, only

Jesus insures Heavenly bliss, the world offers a bottomless pit, you have to decide, are you for Jesus or are you against Jesus

Aug 9th Know your place and remain humble to our Lord and Savior Jesus Christ and our Father who is in Heaven, serve them while they serve you, how, spread the good news, spread the Gospel of Jesus Christ, know who Jesus is and what He did for all of us, know our Father and what He also sacrificed to give you the opportunity to return home to Heaven , this is only possible through the sacrifice of both, it is yours free, know who Jesus is, what He did, and accept Him as your Lord , humble yourself and repent, and you will be saved

Aug 10th When you wake up make Jesus Christ your forethought not your afterthought, He made you a priority in His life, make Him the priority in yours, thank Him this morning for what He has done, Jesus came to this earth to set you free, why stay in bondage, Jesus Christ paid the price, you are free so rejoice and praise Him, He is your salvation, He is the Way, follow Jesus, accept Jesus, today, become a disciple of Jesus

Aug 11th Where do you go when you are lost, go to the feet of Jesus, He cares for you, only He can heal the hurts that are real, He will carry you in times of trouble, His love will never die for you, He will find a way to mend your heart and help you in your time of despair and guide your footsteps through the times when you are lost and can't find your way, He is the way, He has already walked through the paths you are now treading, He is the way, stop and listen for His voice

Aug 12th If you try to achieve something by yourself that is what you may or may not accomplish, if you involve Jesus Christ you will not only achieve victory, you will also gain the blessings that are added to, you will gain direction given through the Holy Spirit, and you will gain the approval of our Heavenly Father, victory through Jesus far outweighs the victories of this world, plan to win with Jesus, include Him and you include the Trinity, you will not lose because with Jesus you cannot lose

Aug 13th The Truth is there is only One Way to succeed in this world, that is to reach out of this world to the Heavenly Throne, there is only one Way to reach out to our Father who is on that Throne, that is through His only Begotten Son Jesus Christ, He is our Intercessor as He sits or stands by our Father Abba to the right on that Heavenly Throne, prayers are answered, they are answered as you need them, every day is a blessing, another chance to get to know our Savior and Lord Jesus Christ, don't let the world blind you, you are a rightful heir through the sacrifices of Jesus Christ

Aug 14th Where is your heart this morning, start at the foot of the cross, your day will be more joyful with Jesus on your side, persecution will come, but you will be prepared with the full armor of God, the flaming arrows of the adversary will not penetrate, make sure you have the spirit of Jesus on your side He will intervene, His love for you is more than any love you will know on this earth, if you don't know Jesus repent and accept the gift of salvation through the actions that Jesus Christ did , providing the only Way to the Father, accept this gift of pure love Jesus offers

Aug 15th Where ever you are today remember Jesus is right beside you, He said He would never leave you nor forsake you, you are special to Him, let Him lead you and you cannot become lost, He knows the Way and He will show you the Way, when you seek Jesus you receive the Trinity, there is no better protection for your daily walk, so walk with Jesus today

Aug 16th How is your relationship with Jesus Christ today, don't rely on a man to tell you of their perception of your relationship, surely you know through the Holy Spirit where your relationship with Jesus stands, man will lead you astray and away from the wonderful relationship that Jesus Christ provides, let Jesus build you up not man, true love comes from those who love you and Jesus has a love for you that cannot be matched here on earth, yes the great deceiver will fool you, don't trust on him, trust in the Truth, trust in Jesus Christ

Aug 17th Do not trust in yourself, trust in the Spirt of Jesus Christ, He will lead you and blessings will abound in your life, you cannot nor ever will be capable of anything without Jesus, He is the manna that nourishes both your physical and spiritual life, He will not ever forsake you, you may forsake Him but repentance from your heart returns you to the relationship with Jesus that brings glory, He said, I will not forsake you or leave you, this is Truth

Aug 18th Do you need strength today, the Lord will provide, the Lord provides all, ask and you will receive, Jesus Christ is our comforter and our strength, He will carry you when needed and walk with you when you think you are alone, once you receive Him as Lord and Savior He is always with you, no matter the situation you find yourself in, He is with you always, in every situation, listen to His words and be thankful, He is always with you, you are not alone

Aug 19th Whatever you run in to ,remember you serve a Risen King, a King who watches over you at all times, call on the name above all names, call on Jesus Christ, you will see results, prayers do not go unanswered, open your heart and eyes, see what happens, you will say that was an answer to a prayer I prayed, Jesus does not forget your prayers, you may, but Jesus will not, don't be surprised when you are blessed, be thankful, you do serve a Risen King, a Savior that knows every hair on your head, One that loves you with a love that will never die or fade, His love was shown on the cross

Aug 20th Who are you following this morning, where do you get your advice from, you need to receive all from the One that gave all, Jesus Christ, He is the Beginning and the End, He has already walked the path that you are on and triumphed over life, and death, rely on the One that knows the Way because He is the Way, make life easier and receive the blessings from the King of Kings Lord of Lords, He is waiting on you, claim the victory that Jesus Christ gives, claim life after death, life in Heaven

Aug 22nd Quit trying to do it all, all by yourself, let go of me and become we, we as in Jesus Christ, we as in the Holy Spirit, we as in our Heavenly Father, if you receive Jesus you receive the other two, it is a package deal, so quit being me and surrender to Jesus Christ, with Jesus there is assurance of eternity, there is assurance of the right path not the wrong path, so repent and have the assurance Jesus Christ brings

Aug 23rd Jesus has already accomplished the will of His Father, the will of our Father who is in Heaven was to save you, this is the reason you must come to His Son, our Risen Savior, Jesus Christ accomplished all and paid your debt, this is why you must go through the Son to reach the Father, seek the Son and you seek the Father and the Spirit, prayer is answered, life's are changed, eternity is granted by the King of Kings, if you don't know Jesus repent and pray, if you do know Jesus as your Savior open your eyes to the blessings He sends daily

Aug 24th Don't put Jesus behinds the scenes in your life, make Jesus a part of the scene in your life, don't be ashamed to announce you are a Christian and that Jesus is a part of your makeup, the most important part of your makeup, Jesus said if you deny Him He will deny you, you belong to His Kingdom where ever you go He will be with you, start with Jesus every day, keep Him close He will not forsake you ever, Jesus said this there for it is Truth, rely on Him and you will become a child of God, you too will call Him Father Abba

Aug 25th Humble yourself and follow Jesus Christ, when you leave Jesus out you are in essence making yourself the leader, so with humility follow Jesus, He will lead you to green pastures, He will lay you by still waters, and He is the Good Shepard, let Jesus lead you, He will not forsake you, the adversary the devil will lead you long enough to forsake you, trust in Jesus Christ and you will be fulfilled, He is the Way, the Truth, and the Life

Aug 26th What are you waiting for, what Jesus Christ gives is free, why do you want to stay in bondage, freedom lies in the acceptance of the actions of Jesus Christ, He paid the price for you, you cannot or never will be able to pay this price, the devil would have you believe that there are other ways to reach the paradise of Heaven, Jesus Christ is the only Way, you have nothing to add or subtract, all you have to do is accept, Jesus loves you and waits on the other side of the door, open it and let Him become part of your life

Aug 27th Why do you make Jesus wait on you, He is already committed to you, you need to commit to Him, let this world go and accept Jesus as your Lord and Savior, He is the Light, why trudge through a world that has no blessings to give when you can receive blessings in abundance, Jesus truly loves you just as you are and waits for you to recognize the Truth, Jesus is the Truth and the Truth will set you free

Aug 28th Why do we think life is so hard, because we try to figure it out on our own, turn to the Author of Life, turn to Jesus Christ, when you turn to Him give Him all, heart, mind, and soul, if you don't life will remain a struggle, quit trying to go through life alone, you will never make it, turn to the One that knows all the mysteries, turn to Jesus Christ, He will not lie to you or deceive you like the father of lies would, Jesus is all Truth, turn to Him and find the greenest pastures

Aug 29th Look around you, you are blessed, you are given what you need by a Risen Savior, one that loves you beyond any love you have ever felt, there are temptations that come your way but Jesus assures you will not be tempted beyond what you can stand, He will always show you away out, you will have a choice, choose Jesus, grow daily in Jesus Christ, know that He will never leave you alone, He is always with you in Spirit, and with His Holy Spirit you are capable, lean on Jesus Christ his burden is light

Aug 30th What are you waiting for, Jesus Christ is knocking now, He is at your door now, is there no urgency, one day the knocking will stop and it will be too late, look what Jesus has already done for you, He came to earth to live as a man, to give you an example of how to live sin free, He was crucified for your sins not His, He conquered death and set the captives free, and was resurrected back to the right side of our Father who is in Heaven to sit in the very Throne Room of Heaven to intervene on our behalf, Jesus Christ is the only Begotten Son of God, don't waste your life on earth, live your life with Jesus Christ, our Savior, He is still knocking

Aug 31st Don't hesitate to pray, pray in Jesus's name, He carries your prayers to our Father, He intercedes, He gives us a voice, Jesus Christ still serves us, look toward the Throne of Heaven Jesus is there waiting to hear from you even today, don't you see how important you are to Him, His love can and will heal your wounds, both physical and spiritual, give Jesus your heart and mind, His love reflects His Fathers, His Fathers love is why He died for us

Sept 1st Our Lord has shown us how to live, He has given us an example, people that don't know Him to have known guidance or boundaries, all they know is the world, so they do the things of the world, share the gospel message, help people that do not know learn of our Lord and Savior Jesus Christ, tell them that through Jesus they too can be set free, free from this world, insure them that they can have victory in Jesus

Sept 2nd Stand up for Jesus, stand up for Jesus, He stands for you in a crisis, Jesus Christ is your intercessor, He does not leave you, don't leave Him, Jesus said if you deny Him He would deny you, this is a relationship, this relationship will stand the test of time, it will last forever, it is permanent, don't forsake or leave Jesus, His love for you is eternal, grasp the hem of His garment in time of crisis and times of happiness, pray for each other through Jesus, He will carry your prayers to our Heavenly Father, love the Trinity and love each other

www.ingramcontent.com/pod-product-compliance
Lightning Source LLC
Chambersburg PA
CBHW061427040426
42450CB00007B/932